SCRABBLE®BRAND

Crossword Game

Word Puzzles

Puzzle creators: Cihan Altay, Liz Barker, Chris Bolton, George Bredehorn, Myles Callum, Philip Carter, Clarity Media, Jeff Cockrell, Don Cook, Jeanette Dall, Caroline Delbert, Josie Faulkner, Holli Fort, Erich Friedman, Luke Haward, Rod Hines, Marilynn Huret, William I. Johnston, Lloyd King, David Millar, Michael Moreci, Alan Olschwang, Fred Piscop, Emily Rice, Stephen Ryder, Pete Sarjeant, Terry Stickels, Fraser Simpson, Startdl Puzzles, Terry Stickels, Nicole Sulgit, Wayne Robert Williams, John Wilmes

Puzzle illustrators: Helem An, Chris Gattorna, Elizabeth Gerber, Robin Humer, Nicole H. Lee, Anna Lender, Shavan Spears, Jen Torche

 North American SCRABBLE® Players Association

Special thanks to the North American SCRABBLE ® Players Association (NASPA) for select strategy tips and facts. For more information on NASPA, visit their website: www.scrabbleplayers.org.

ISBN: 978-1-68022-100-8

Manufactured in China.

8 7 6 5 4 3 2 1

 Publications International, Ltd.

Crossword Twist

Fit the given words into the crossword grid. Be careful with your selections though — more words are provided than are needed.

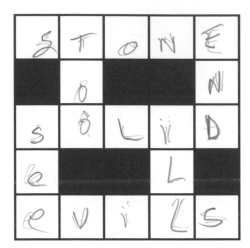

END
EVILS
ILL
SEE
SOLID
STONE
TOO
TOW

Finely Fit

In this miniature crossword, the clues are listed randomly and are numbered for convenience only. It is up to you to figure out the placement of the 9 answers. To help you, we've inserted one letter in the grid, and this is the only occurrence of that letter in the completed puzzle.

CLUES

1. Tie up, as the Thanksgiving turkey
2. Finished
3. Throat dangler
4. Waikiki wingding
5. Thanksgiving side dish
6. King's domain
7. Like Swiss cheese
8. Building extensions
9. "The _____ Locker"

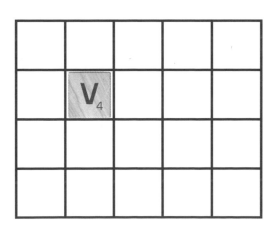

Word for Bird

It's 2 jumbles in one! First, unscramble the 7 letters under each row of squares to form Scrabble words. When you've done this, unscramble the letters running down each column in the blackened boxes to reveal 2 more words.

| E | D | I | T | I | O | N |

I I N E O T D

RUGNEYO

| K | P | U | D | O | L | A |

LVRAOII

EDPOALT

| K | I | N | D | R | E | D |

NRIEKDD

NUTIPAO

T E R M

BINGO-PRONE TILES:
A group of tiles that are likely to produce a bingo. Often used to describe a player's set of three to six tiles just before drawing his or her replacement tiles.

Makes a Kind of Sense

Find the hidden quip by using the letters directly below each of the blank squares. Each letter is used only once. A black square indicates the end of a word.

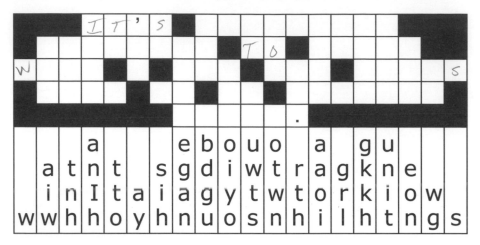

Fabulous Cryptids

No Loch Ness monster or Bigfoot here, but these mostly amiable beasts are indeed fabulous – that is, they're creatures of fable. Do you remember what they're called? Decipher the anagrams.

1. COIN URN *unicorn*

2. DOG RAN *Dragon*

3. AIM TO RUN

4. RAN CUTE

5. I'M DREAM

6. GIN RIFF *Griffin*

D₂ I₁ D₂ YOU KNOW?

Y₄ O₁ U₁ K₅ N₁ O₁ W₄?

The very top SCRABBLE players average 35 or more points per turn, not counting exchanges.

Answers on page 172.

Put Your Finger On It

Use the clues to solve the puzzle. When complete, the circled letters will spell out a mystery word.

①M	A	N	O	R
②S	Ⓐ	I	N	T
③I	N	Ⓝ	E	R
④T	U	L	Ⓘ	P
⑤M	U	S	I	Ⓒ

ACROSS
1. Grand home
2. Papal nominee
3. Not outer
4. Dutch bulb
5. Dulcet tones

⑥Ⓤ	⑦P	⑧S	⑨E	⑩T
N	Ⓡ	A	I	R
D	A	Ⓘ	R	E
E	N	L	Ⓢ	A
R	K	S	T	Ⓣ

DOWN
6. Not over
7. Practical joke
8. Travels on water
9. Winner's place
10. Trick or _____

Mystery-word clue:
Salon employee

manicurist

Shall I Compare Thee...

Each rack of seven letters below forms exactly one valid seven-letter bingo word. Unscramble them to find the bingo, then find words with six, five, four, three, and two letters each to complete the puzzle.

Word Jigsaw

Fit the pieces into the frame to form Scrabble wordss reading across and down. There's no need to rotate the pieces; they'll fit as shown, with each piece used once.

1.
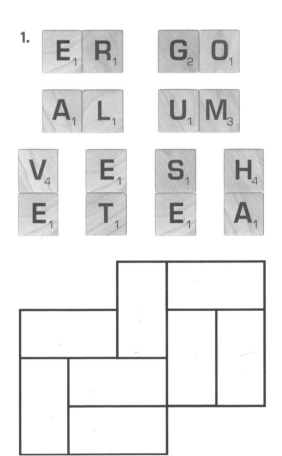

2.
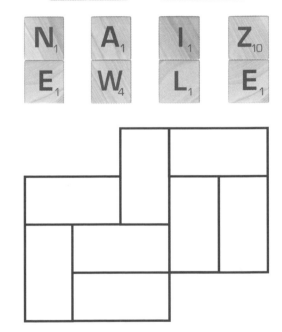

T₁ I₁ P₃

Most casual SCRABBLE players don't ever exchange tiles, but it can be to your benefit if you're consistently making low-scoring plays.

Answers on page 172.

Spoken Well

Four 6-letter words, all of which revolve around the same theme, have been jumbled. Unscramble each word, and write the answer in the accompanying space. Next, transfer the letters in the shaded boxes into the shaded keyword space, and unscramble the 8-letter word that goes with the theme.

Hint: The theme for this puzzle is "spread the word."

LEGSOP

PLEACH

MRNOSE

STRIPE

Answers on page 172.

Better to Give

Every word in the list on the facing page is contained within the group of letters. Words can be found in a straight line horizontally, vertically, or diagonally. They may be read either forward or backward.

AID
BEQUEST
CHARITY
CONTRIBUTION
DONATION
ENDOWMENT
FUNDING
GENEROSITY
GIFT
GRANT
HELP
LEGACY
NONPROFIT
PATRONAGE
PHILANTHROPY
SCHOLARSHIP

```
C O N T R I B U T I O N R
Y C A G E L Y B W N F P J
Y W M F H T E A O U I Y T
T L E F S Q I N N H C M X
I H C G U D P D S J E V E
S C X E A R I R H E L P N
O G S D O N A T I O N C D
R T I F G L O U U G T H O
E A I F O G S R L E X A W
N T W H T X L H T M J R M
E Y C Z M L Q B B A M I E
G S Z G R A N T B F P T N
P H I L A N T H R O P Y T
```

Wedge the Words

Fit the words into the grid reading across and down. One word will appear twice. Two letters have already been given.

AISLE	~~RISKS~~
INKER	~~STAIR~~
INLET	STRIP
~~PEERS~~	TWINE
RESTS	

Rather Numerous

Spell a 10-letter word by moving between adjacent letters. Every letter will be used at least once, but no letter will be used consecutively. Begin at any letter.

Ways to Move

Fill in each white square with a different letter so a trio of related words is formed.

Answers on page 173.

Across and Down

In this miniature crossword, the clues are listed randomly and are numbered for convenience only. It is up to you to figure out the placement of the 9 answers. To help you, we've inserted one letter in the grid, and this is the only occurrence of that letter in the completed puzzle.

Clues

1. Beaming
2. Hydrant hookup
3. Urged, with "on"
4. Wide-eyed
5. Chest-thumping

6. Got behind
7. Lasso loop
8. Drain obstruction
9. Leo's locks

Alphabet Menagerie

Enter every letter of the alphabet into the grid. Letters are connected horizontally, vertically, or diagonally from A to Z. Use the clue to fill in the circles and help complete the grid.

Clue: Pets

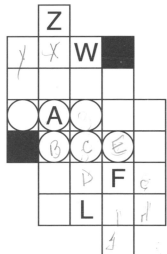

In a timed game, neither player's time continues during challenges, rule disputes, or score verifications.

There's An Art to It

Use the clues to solve the puzzle. When complete, the circled letters will spell out a mystery word.

①N	O	R	T	H
²R	Ⓐ	C	E	D
³		Ⓘ		
⁴S	E	A	Ⓛ	S
⁵B	E	N	I	Ⓐ P

ACROSS

1. Not south
2. Sped competitively
3. Grab
4. Marine mammals
5. Nonmalignant tumor

⁶Ⓞ	⁷	⁸T	⁹Ⓖ	¹⁰M
N	Ⓛ	W	R	O
i		Ⓘ	S	U
N		R	Ⓢ	T
G		L	H	Ⓗ

DOWN

6. In debt
7. Angle
8. Baton move
9. Auto collision
10. Oral cavity

Mystery phrase clue:
Finger deco

Paint By Numbers

Each rack of seven letters below forms exactly one valid seven-letter bingo word. Unscramble them to find the bingo, then find words with six, five, four, three, and two letters each to complete the puzzle.

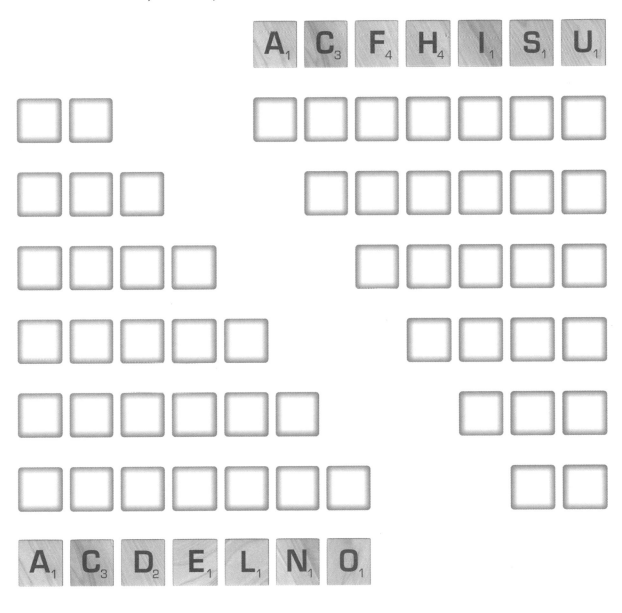

Code-doku

Solve this puzzle just as you would a Sudoku puzzle. Use deductive logic to complete the grid so that each row, each column, and both diagonals contain each of the letters of the word MOUTH in some order. The solution is unique. We've inserted 6 letters to get you started.

Forward Thinking

These seven letters spell exactly one valid seven-letter Scrabble word. Can you find it?

Answers on page 173.

Flying High

Unscramble the names of these common birds, then use the numbered squares to solve the second puzzle, a related idiom.

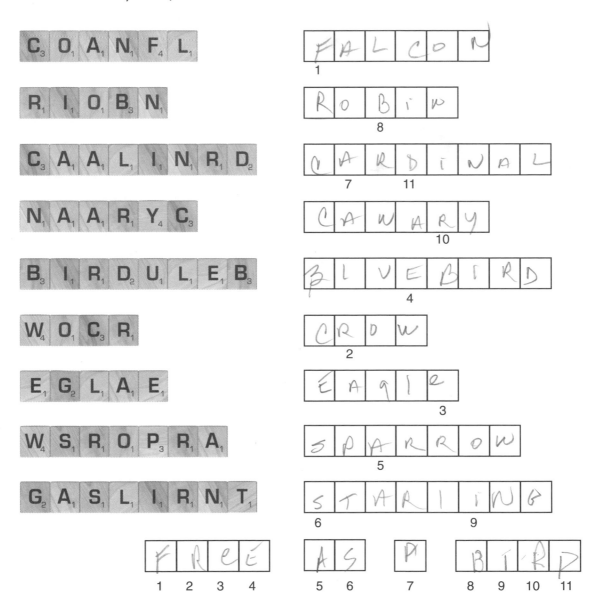

COANFL → FALCON (1)

RIOBN → ROBIN (8)

CAALINRD → CARDINAL (7, 11)

NAARYC → CANARY (10)

BIRDULEB → BLUEBIRD (4)

WOCR → CROW (2)

EGLAE → EAGLE (3)

WSROPRA → SPARROW (5)

GASLIRNT → STARLING (6, 9)

FREE (1 2 3 4) AS (5 6) P (7) BIRD (8 9 10 11)

SCRABBLE

W₄ O₁ R₁ D₂

Split Decisions

Fill in each set of empty cells with letters that will create Scrabble words reading both across and down. Letters may repeat within a single set. We've completed one set to get you started.

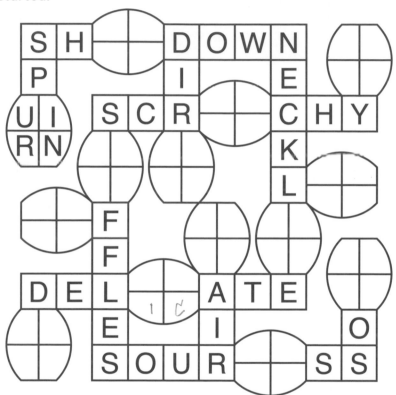

Scrambled Letters

Below is a common everyday word, only scrambled. The G and the Y are the first and last letters, but not necessarily in that order. Can you figure out the word?

Y — HIGO / CARE / LLAP — G

Answers on page 174.

A to Z

Enter every letter of the alphabet into the grid. Letters are connected horizontally, vertically, or diagonally from A to Z. Use the clue to fill in the circles and help complete the grid.

Clue: Extremities

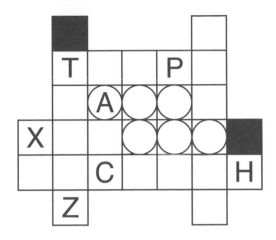

It's in the Drawer

This puzzle functions exactly like an anagram with an added step: In addition to being scrambled, each word or phrase below is missing the same letter. Discover the missing letter, then unscramble the words. When you do, you'll reveal 4 kitchen utensils.

GREAT   **NEON CAPE**

NASTIER   **SPACE GIRLS**

Get Moving!

Fill in each white square with a different letter so a trio of related words is formed.

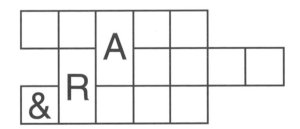

"IRATE on the board? Keep your eye out for the P, matey!"

—Curran Eggerston, 2013 Edmonton, AB Champion

Answers on page 174.

A Spot of Starch

Use the clues to solve the puzzle. When complete, the circled letters will spell out a mystery word.

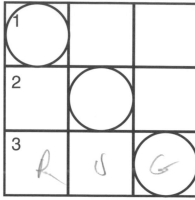

ACROSS
1. To place
2. Negative
3. Floor cover

DOWN
4. Perform
5. Eat (past tense)
6. What person?

Mystery word clue:
Edible tuber

Scratch It Out

These seven letters spell exactly one valid seven-letter Scrabble word. Can you find it?

C₃ C₃ E₁ H₄ I₁ N₁ K₅

Answers on page 174.

Circular Words

Find 2 eight-letter words that are synonyms. Words are found by combining one letter from each circle moving in a clockwise direction. Each word starts in a different circle and each letter is used only once.

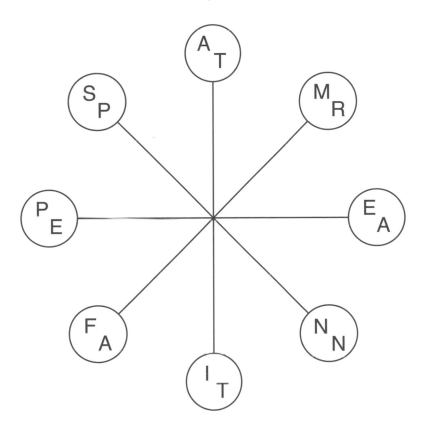

TERM

CHALLENGE: When the opponent thinks a play is not acceptable. Whenever there is a challenge, someone loses exactly one turn.

SCRABBLE

Add-a-Letter

This is a standard word search with a twist: For each word in the list, you must add one letter to form a new word, which you will then search for in the grid. For example: If the listed word is CARTON, you'd search for CARTOON; if the listed word is OTTER, you might have to search for HOTTER or POTTER. The words can be found in a straight line horizontally, vertically, or diagonally, and may read forward or backward.

BEAD	GLACE	SAKE
BOTHER	GROW	SHINE
BREK	HOSE	SICK
CANE	MAKER	SOON
CEMENT	MATH	SOOTHED
COOKED	PACED	SORT
CRIMP	PONE	STAVE
CURE	PRICE	STOKE
DEAL	RAID	TALK
DEBT	RELAY	TRIES
ELECT	RIDDLE	VERSION
EXTANT	ROGUE	
FLING	RUSED	

```
C J T I B E D L R E K R A M G
S M O O T H E D S C R I M P H
G L A N C E K C L E M E N T S
G C U R V E C L I J X K D E T
B R E A K S A N C G W A R S A
R T Q E H C P D K R U N A S L
O R G R E O T C E L E S E T K
T O I D S L S P D K P Y B A H
H N S W W E L S T R O K E R C
E S O O X A V E R S I O N V T
R O R T Y K G N I Y L F R E A
N G A R N H O R S E O N A C M
P N P R I N C E R U S T E D J
T R I B E S E L D D I R G H N
O N D K R B R O G U E N O H P
```

T I P

The longest word you can find isn't always the highest scoring.

From A to Z

Use every letter in the alphabet once to fill the blanks in this puzzle.

Answers on page 174.

Addagram

This puzzle functions exactly like an anagram with an added step: In addition to being scrambled, each word below is missing the same letter. Discover the missing letter, then unscramble the words.

1. You'll reveal a weather phenomenon, a state of delirium, a synonym for "refuge," and a word describing a central support.

2. You'll reveal a craftsperson, a receptacle, a liquid produced by plants, and a synonym for "interweave."

One Word Leads to Another

Place 3 letters in the middle squares that will complete one word and start another. For example, TAR would complete GUI TAR GET.

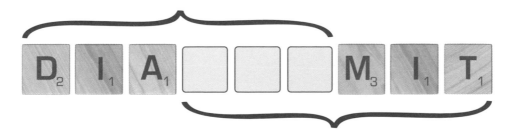

Answers on page 174.

Find the Perfect Fit

Fit the words into the grid reading across and down. Each word is used once.

ANNA	HOUR
CHASE	OUNCE
CHOP	PRATS
EYES	SECT
HONEY	

Combing for Clues

Answer each clue with a 6-letter word. Write the words in a clockwise direction around the numerals in the grid. Words overlap each other and may start in any of the spaces around the numerals. We've placed some letters to get you started.

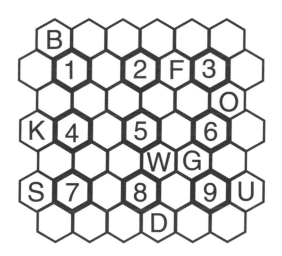

1. Incorporate
2. Envelop
3. Blundered
4. Servile follower
5. Luxuriate
6. Courting
7. Climbed
8. Seized with fingernails
9. Spice

Answers on page 175.

Put It All Together

Use the clues to solve the puzzle. When complete, the circled letters will spell out a mystery word.

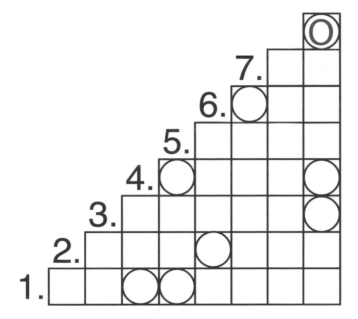

ACROSS

1. Complete outfit
2. Green gem
3. Pearls, diamonds, and rubies
4. 'Fuss up'
5. Coffee stand
6. A trilby
7. In the event that

Mystery word: _____

Classical Talent

Unscramble the letters in each line to solve the puzzle. The words cross on a letter that they share.

M
Y
O
Y
T S O H R R A E C
P
N
S

A Cut Above

Each rack of seven letters below forms exactly one valid seven-letter bingo word. Unscramble them to find the bingo, then find words with six, five, four, three, and two letters each to complete the puzzle.

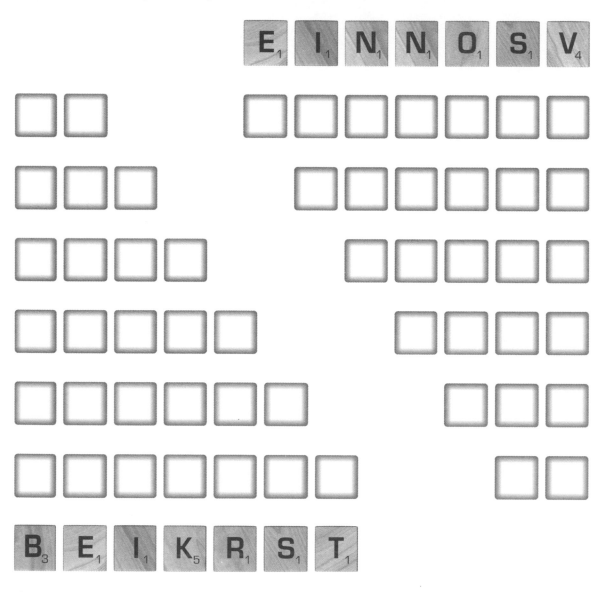

Wise Words

Cryptograms are messages in substitution code. Break the code to read the message. For example, THE SMART CAT might become FVO QWGDF JGF if F is substituted for T, V for H, O for E, and so on. The code is different for each cryptogram.

JIRY IB VR GCQ EIFGE – ZSQH ZQ CQGMS G MQCYGAH GUQ ZQ EAWQ YI RYAMW YI AY.

YZV YZPGWB KCBY UVCUSV JQGY YC AGCJ QTV GCGV CM YZVPT IFBPGVBB.

EYQRUEX UC UAMYCCUJSL QY QRL ABE ZRY PYLC EYQ RBGL QY PY UQ RUACLSV.

EFVAUVAY GBOO VX GVXB; SOCAAVAY GBOO VX GVXBN; MH-VAY GBOO VX GVXBXE CAM PBXE HR COO.

JIX LZY BFFT JIXK WFZC ZMIAF NZRFK OS JIX WIDC JIXK LWOY XT.

YBWWRYY NY QJGPNJV ZIR KNEERMRJWR HRZPRRJ WGM-JRMNJV SRGSTR LJK VRZZNJV ZIRO NJ DGBM WGMJRM.

HOT SPOTS: These are squares or areas on the board that have excellent bonus-scoring opportunities, like Triple Letter Squares or Double Word Squares adjacent to vowels.

Birthday Food

Travel in sequence through the puzzle from the left side to the right, using each numbered clue to determine the correct word. Connect adjacent words together with a common letter to proceed through the maze. Some letters are already given. The first and last words tie into the title.

1. Ply (as plywood)	**8. Tasty**	**15. Not casual**
2. Place to put cash	**9. Horned animal**	**16. Ill**
3. Kitchen bug	**10. Retain**	**17. Round handle**
4. Tubular food	**11. Rare and valuable**	**18. Mechanized limb**
5. Au	**12. Decadent**	**19. Hardened (as mud)**
6. Mom's mate	**13. Parameter**	
7. Meaningless work	**14. Arbor**	

Answers on page 175.

Lots of Air

Use the clues to solve the puzzle. When complete, the circled letters will spell out a mystery word.

ACROSS
1. Floating craft
2. Metric weight measure
3. Thermal energy
4. Suspend

DOWN
5. Small, rough particle
6. Silicon oxide granule
7. Market place
8. Small pie

Mystery word clue:
Boaster

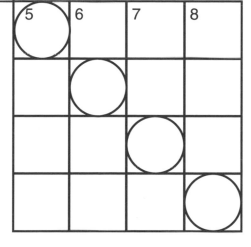

ALPHAGRAM: The alphabetic arrangement of a group of letters.

Answers on page 175.

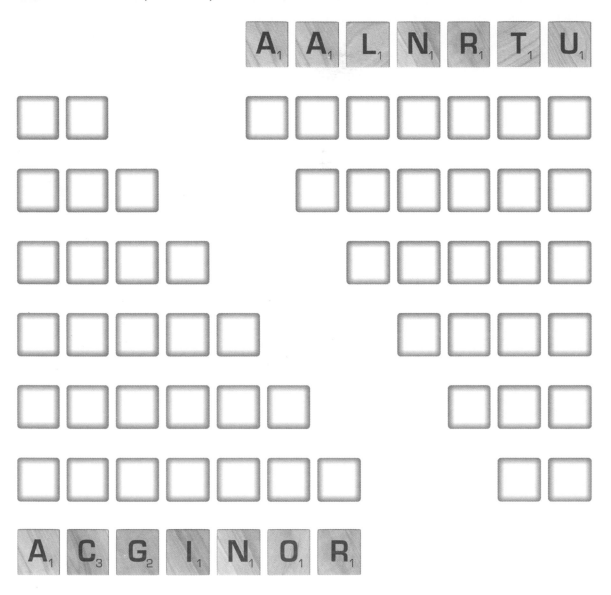

Moral Fiber

Each rack of seven letters below forms exactly one valid seven-letter bingo word. Unscramble them to find the bingo, then find words with six, five, four, three, and two letters each to complete the puzzle.

A A L N R T U

A C G I N O R

Word Ladder

Use the clues to change just one letter on each line to go from the top word to the bottom word. Do not change the order of the letters. You must have a Scrabble word at each step.

1. DRUNK

_____ the body of a human or tree

_____ informal thud

_____ to express gratitude

_____ haunch

_____ hit on the fanny

_____ a reek in the past

STAND

2. BRINE

_____ seven of them for seven brothers

_____ a group of lions

_____ to hold something dear

PRIME

Anagrams

Fill in the blanks in each sentence below with words that are anagrams (rearrangements of the same letters) of one another.

1. My _____ can _____ numbers better than yours.

2. _____ is my favorite month to eat a _____.

3. When Dad found out he'd eaten a _____ fish, our home was a battle

site for the third world _____.

4. The _____ of a lion's day is spent in the _____.

5. Lao-Tse never _____ until the _____ was poured.

Answers on page 176.

Crazy Mixed-Up Letters

How many 7-letter words can you make using these letters? You must use all 7 letters in each word.

The Perfect Way to Say It

Below is a group of words that, when properly arranged in the blanks, reveal a quote from Ralph Waldo Emerson.

PATH GO TRAIL IS NOT INSTEAD AND

"Do _____ _____ where the _____ may lead, go _____ where there _____ no path _____ leave a _____."

Answer the Homophone

You are given 2 words. Your objective is to come up with a set of homophones (words that sound alike but are spelled differently) that would either precede or follow each of these words. For example, GUITAR and SECOND would be BASS and BASE.

CIVIL, LAST

Answers on page 176.

Classical Music Makers

Fill in the blank spaces as you would a crossword puzzle. The theme – or title – of the puzzle might appear to be ambiguous, but it should suggest a category of words that, when linked together, will complete the puzzle.

For example, HOLE IN ONE might suggest DOUGHNUTS. Or, it might suggest GOLF, which would lead to the words CLUB, IRON, TEE, etc. But all of these words have a common theme. Notice that a few letters are already in place, and some of the words intersect – adding to the mystery, and the fun, of finding the solution.

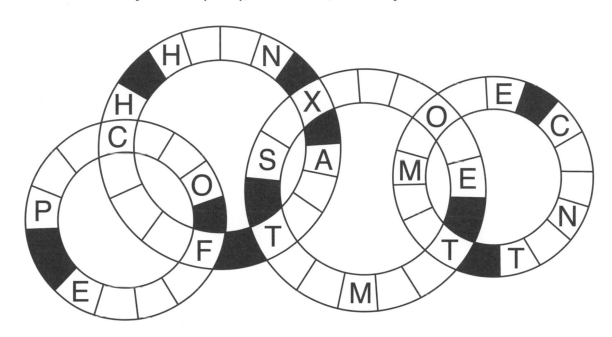

T I P

Despite being worth 10 points, the Q can be bad because it can be so difficult to use. If you have no U, play it as soon as you can, even if it's for very few points.

Answers on page 176.

Add-a-Letter

This is a standard word search with a twist: For each word in the list, you must add one letter to form a new word, which you will then search for in the grid. For example: If the listed word is CARTON, you'd search for CARTOON; if the listed word is OTTER, you might have to search for HOTTER or POTTER. The words can be found in a straight line horizontally, vertically, or diagonally, and may read forward or backward.

BARER	HOPED	SOON
BASTING	HOSE	STARED
BATH	INKING	STEAK
BUSHED	OVEREAT	STUDY
CARFUL	PARED	TRACE
DEIGN	QUIT	VALE
EIGHTY	RANCH	WATER
ENTER	REUSE	WAVER
FAME	SALE	ZONE
FILL	SALLOW	
FLAY	SELVES	
FORTH	SHILL	
GALLEY	SICKLE	

```
U G C E N T E R B R A N C H U
I F A O W A I T E R S M U S F
S N O L Q P B X S S T A T E L
S W K U L L I R H S L I B V A
S T I L R E V I A W C D A L M
S E U F I T R A L K P E R E E
T T C R O N H Y L D W P B H N
F A A A D Q G E O V H P E S W
D L E R R Y X I W B E O R I S
E O A H T E M H S E A H R F T
H I Z K R E F U S E I T J S R
S R U O Y E D U E Z D G C A E
U U S X N J V L L I R F H H A
L P A R K E D O E C N A R T K
B L D Q W C B O A S T I N G Y
```

T₁ I₁ P₃

If you can't shut down a dangerous opening, consider creating a second one. One of the two should be available to you on your next turn.

Let's Puzzle!

Follow the arrows to solve each clue and complete the grid.

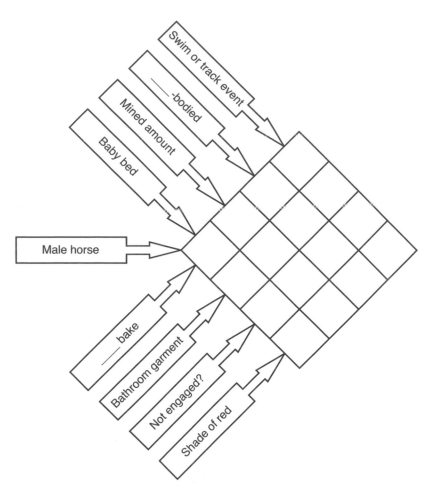

Swim or track event

___-bodied

Mined amount

Baby bed

Male horse

___ bake

Bathroom garment

Not engaged?

Shade of red

T₁ E₁ R₁ M₃

VOWEL DUMP: A valid play with a high proportion of vowels to help balance a rack with too many vowels.

Answers on page 176.

Pinwheel

This pinwheel holds 12 six-letter words that answer the clues below. The last 3 letters of each word are the same as the first 3 letters of the next, and the last 3 letters of Word 12 are the same as the first 3 letters of Word 1. Start each word in a square with a number and work from left to right. We've put in the answer to Clue No. 1 to get you started.

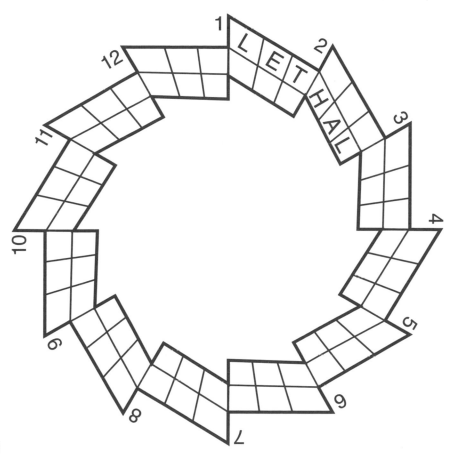

CLUES

1. Deadly
2. Make holy
3. Making moolike noises
4. Actress Bergman
5. Taken for a trot
6. Of the teeth
7. Special aptitude
8. Main course
9. Walked as if drunk
10. Accounts book
11. Hamster-like pet
12. Assign quarters to soldiers

Answers on page 176.

SCRABBLE

W O R D

Seamless Spiral

This puzzle works exactly like a crossword, only without the divisions between words. In fact, some words blend into one another, so solving one clue will help you solve another. Numbers indicate the boxes answers occupy.

1	2	3	4	5	6	7	8	9
32	33	34	35	36	37	38	39	10
31	56	57	58	59	60	61	40	11
30	55	72	73	74	75	62	41	12
29	54	71	80		76	63	42	13
28	53	70	79	78	77	64	43	14
27	52	69	68	67	66	65	44	15
26	51	50	49	48	47	46	45	16
25	24	23	22	21	20	19	18	17

Answers on page 175.

1-4. Take a break

1-8. Make racket repairs

5-11. Sounding a bell

8-13. Snap cookie

11-16. Verbal noun

14-19. Disassembled

17-23. Burdensome

20-27. Kicking out of bed

24-30. Causes an itch

28-33. Classroom topic

31-36. Type of poem

34-40. Interconnected system

37-43. Training routine

41-46. Wall socket

44-49. Deadly

47-52. Divides in two

50-56. Faint trace

53-57. Woods on a golf course

55-60. Pet rodent

58-64. Evading payment

61-67. Realm

65-69. Some stadium tops

68-73. Third-party contract

70-76. Wrecker's tool

74-80. Price cut

77-80. Make headway

It's Superlative

These seven letters spell exactly one valid seven-letter Scrabble word. Can you find it?

Answers on page 176.

Word Ladder

Change just one letter on each line to go from the top word to the bottom word.
Do not change the order of the letters. You must have a Scrabble word at each step.

1. PINK

———

———

———

ROSE

2. JADE

———

——— not narrow

———

———

RING

3. COOK

———

——— cut meat

———

———

CHEF

4. FOOD

———

———

———

MENU

TWO(S)-TO-MAKE-THREE: Two-letter words that take a third letter placed in front or back to form a three-letter word. AN is a two-to-make-three: BAN, CAN, AND, ANT, etc.

Answers on page 176.

Borrowed Words

The words in the box below contain Scrabble words that originated in different languages. Use the words to fill in the blanks.

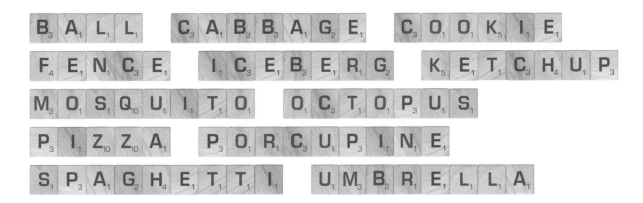

BALL   CABBAGE   COOKIE
FENCE   ICEBERG   KETCHUP
MOSQUITO   OCTOPUS
PIZZA   PORCUPINE
SPAGHETTI   UMBRELLA

1. _____ from two Greek words meaning "eight foot."

2. _____ from two Latin words meaning "spiny pig."

3. _____ from an Italian word meaning "pie."

4. _____ from a Dutch word meaning "mountain of ice."

5. _____ from a Latin word meaning "head."

6. _____ from an Italian word meaning "string."

7. _____ from a Greek word meaning "to throw."

8. _____ from a Malay word meaning "fish sauce."

9. _____ from a Latin word meaning "to keep away."

10. _____ from a Dutch word meaning "cake."

11. _____ from a Spanish word meaning "fly."

12. _____ from a Latin word meaning "shade."

Answers on page 176.

Addagram

This puzzle functions exactly like an anagram with an added step: In addition to being scrambled, each word below is missing the same letter. Discover the missing letter, then unscramble the words.

1. You'll reveal a wading bird, a precious metal, a word meaning "humor," and a word meaning "residue."

2. You'll reveal a sport, an herb, a carpet term, and a group of people or companies.

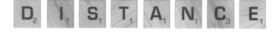

Link and Lock

Place 3 letters in the middle squares that will complete one word and start another. For example, TAR would complete GUI TAR GET.

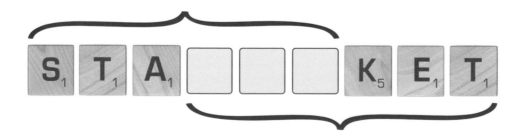

Answers on page 177.

Hone Your Rhymes

Each clue leads to a 2- or 3-word answer that rhymes, such as BIG PIG or STABLE TABLE. The numbers in parentheses after the clue give the number of letters in each word. For example, "Cookware taken from the oven (3, 3)" would be HOT POT.

1. It holds a national symbol (4,3): _____

2. A problem with a popular side served at a holiday picnic (4,4): _____

3. A piece of the action in some seasonal entertainment (4,5): _____

4. Something you never expect to see on July 4th (5,4): _____

5. Complications in the scheduling of the various holiday speeches (7,4): _____

6. He recites poetry throughout the holiday patio party (8,4): _____

7. A competition of politicians from various places in honor of the holiday (6,7): _____

8. A large group that marches in a holiday spectacle (6,7): _____

9. It's now over 235 years (6,8): _____

10. Glee when the interminable speeches finally ended (7,7): _____

11. The Major Leagues new slogan in an effort to get better attendance at the holiday games (8,3,3): _____

12. Where the flag carriers train (5,5,4): _____

13. Spice up a holiday picnic condiment (9,6): _____

14. A job for Thomas Jefferson (11,8): _____

15. A part of that declaration (12,8): _____

Find the Younger One

Spell a 10-letter word by moving between adjacent letters. Every letter will be used at least once, but no letter will be used consecutively. Begin at any letter.

Answers on page 177.

Plus Code

Each set of letters represents a 5-letter word. To decipher each word, move either forward or backward in the alphabet the same number of letters for each letter given in a word. For example, if you move ahead 3 letters from each letter in ALQ, you'll discover the word DOT. (A + 3 letters = D; L + 3 letters = O; Q + 3 letters = T). When counting letters, keep in mind that the end of the alphabet connects with the beginning (Z + 4 letters = D). Use the alphabet line below to keep track of the number of moves you make.

1. EJKNF _____
2. NGCXU _____
3. ZQZIO _____
4. ITUFQ _____
5. JGEIG _____

6. NTSNH _____
7. BLUFJ _____
8. SHGXL _____
9. HFHEC _____
10. GCGPI _____

A₁ B₃ C₃ D₂ E₁ F₄ G₂ H₄ I₁ J₈ K₅ L₁ M₃
N₁ O₁ P₃ Q₁₀ R₁ S₁ T₁ U₁ V₄ W₄ X₈ Y₄ Z₁₀

Anagrammed to Homonyms

An anagram is a word made of the rearranged letters of another word (as in MADE and DAME). Homonyms have the same sound but different spellings (as in HERE and HEAR). Anagram each pair of words below to form a pair of homonyms.

EARL _____ LEER

KEEL _____ LAKE

LEAN _____ NAIL

MATE _____ TEEM

OARS _____ ROSE

Answers on page 177.

The Fruit Vendor's Cart

Help a fruit vendor with an overturned fruit cart gather all the fruit and put it back on his cart. The list below shows each kind of fruit he had on his cart. The grid represents the only way the cart can be organized to hold all the fruit. Put each word in place so the vendor can get on his way.

APPLE	FIG	PEACH
APRICOT	GRAPE	PEAR
AVOCADO	LEMON	STRAWBERRY
BANANA	LIME	TANGERINE
CHERRY	ORANGE	

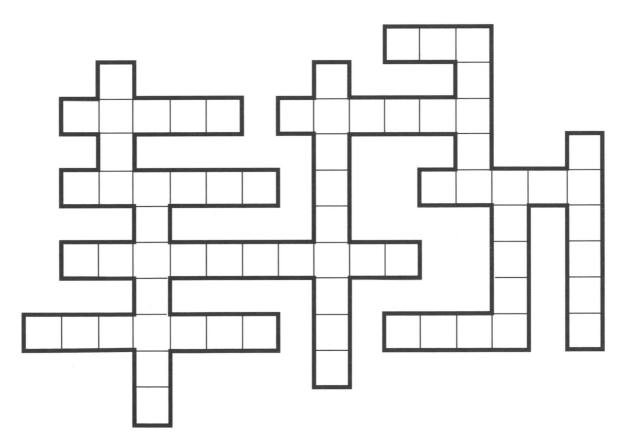

Answers on page 177.

In a Stew

It's dinner time! Can you unscramble the ingredients for the stew?

R₁ A₁ C₃ T₁ O₁ R₁   _____

R₁ U₁ P₃ I₁ N₁ T₁   _____

A₁ T₁ A₁ S₁ P₃   _____

T₁ O₁ O₁ T₁ A₁ P₃   _____

S₁ E₁ I₁ N₁ A₁ S₁ O₁ N₁ G₂   _____

K₅ E₁ L₁ E₁   _____

C₃ E₁ N₁ I₁ C₃ H₄ K₅   _____

C₃ R₁ Y₄ L₁ E₁ E₁   _____

When looking for 7- and 8-letter words, start by seeing
which common prefixes and suffixes you can make.

Answers on page 177.

Rhyme Time

Each clue leads to a 2-word answer that rhymes, such as BIG PIG or STABLE TABLE. The numbers in parentheses after the clue give the number of letters in each word.

1. Old-fashioned watch (4, 4): _____

2. A dive over the line for a touchdown (4, 4): _____

3. Overheated college residence (4, 4): _____

4. Swindle on the tracks (4, 4): _____

5. Swine utensil (4, 4): _____

6. Antique-store purchase (4, 5): _____

7. A most impressive bird of prey (5, 5): _____

8. Sugar cookie (5, 5): _____

9. Clique within the cast (6, 5): _____

10. In-crowd's favorite flick (6, 5): _____

11. Temporary crown (6, 6): _____

12. Roach-race timer (7, 5): _____

Every Letter Plus Two Numbers

Enter every letter of the alphabet into the grid. Letters are connected horizontally, vertically, or diagonally from A to Z. Use the clue to fill in the circles and help complete the grid.

Clue: Numbers

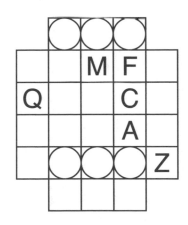

Word Ladder

Change just one letter on each line to go from the top word to the bottom word. Do not change the order of the letters. You must have a Scrabble word or a name at each step.

1. HATE

_____

_____

_____

LOVE

2. DOVE

_____ profound affection

_____ traditional knowledge

_____ to tempt

_____ to wait secretly

LARK

Where Are the Animals?

Find the names of 2 animals in each group of letters. The letters for each animal are in their proper order.

1. DOCAGT _____ _____

2. SEKLUNKK _____ _____

3. DEOWERL _____ _____

4. FOSNAXKE _____ _____

5. WHOORLSEF _____ _____

6. RELAEBPHABINTT _____ _____

7. TILIGONER _____ _____

8. MEONAGKLEYE _____ _____

9. SWEHALALE _____ _____

10. PEAREROLT _____ _____

Answers on page 177.

Our Loopy Lingo

Rearrange the tiles to produce a head-scratching question. **Hint:** It starts with the word "If."

N D S	HA	D E	ONE	HA	V E	D D S
I F	L B	YOU	D G	TH	E T	F O
OF	UT	AT	EM ,	RID	OF	W H
A N	YOU	VE ?	DO	A B	AL	UNC
A N	H O

What Did He Say?

Below is a group of words that, when properly arranged in the blanks, reveal a quote from Saul Bellow.

FOUND DISTRACTIONS YOURSELF HAPPINESS BE YOU OTHER

"_____ can only _____ _____ if _____ can free _____ of all _____ _____."

Know Your ABCs

Fill in each individual block with the letters A, B, and C. No letter should be adjacent to itself — horizontally or vertically — between blocks.

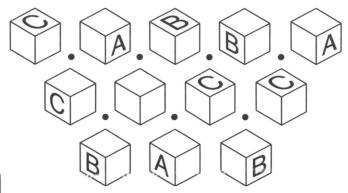

Fair Ball

Find the hidden phrase by using the letters directly below each of the blank squares. Each letter is used only once. A black square indicates the end of a word.

Answers on page 178.

All Squared

Complete the word square at right using 4 words that mean, in this order: get ready for; big; a jungle cat; and the back of a ship.

S	A	L	T	S
A				
L				
T				
S				

A Nonstop State

Fill in each white square with a different letter so a trio of related words is formed.

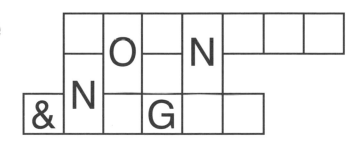

It's Political

These seven letters spell exactly one valid seven-letter Scrabble word. Can you find it?

Answers on page 178.

Play Ball!

What words, formed by different arrangements of 5 letters, can be used to complete the sentences below?

1. A pitcher's _____ is based on how well he can _____.

2. After the slugger hit the ball, propelling it high _____, he watched it _____ over the rightfield fence.

3. The sports writer _____ all the players involved in the recent _____.

4. The potential base-stealer who _____ when taking a lead will need more than a well-executed _____ if he hopes to succeed.

5. A fast base-runner may _____ at _____ one base per game.

6. The base-runner barely mussed a _____ in his uniform when he slid into home _____.

Nip to It

Use the clues to solve the puzzle. When complete, the circled letters will spell out a mystery word.

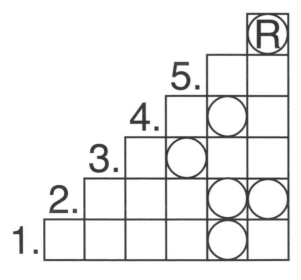

ACROSS
1. Remove from the surface
2. Arena spectators
3. Goal support
4. Goal material
5. "_____ no!"

Mystery word: _____

Answers on page 178.

Exterior Design

Each rack of seven letters below forms exactly one valid seven-letter bingo word. Unscramble them to find the bingo, then find words with six, five, four, three, and two letters each to complete the puzzle.

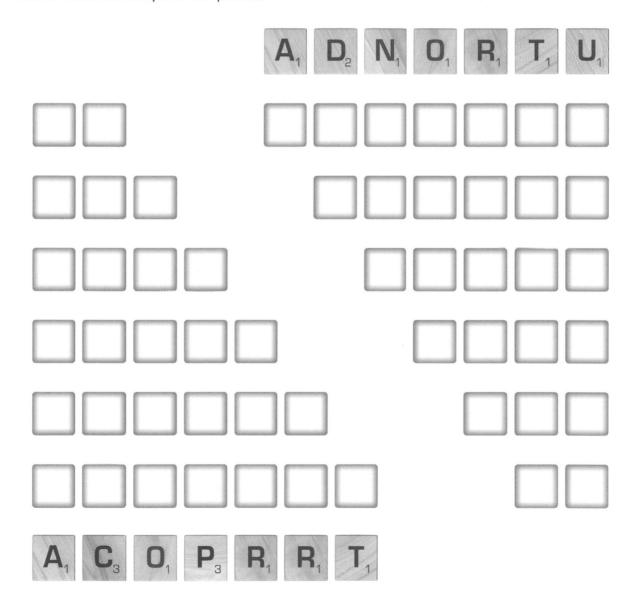

Elevator Words

Like an elevator, words move up and down the "floors" of this puzzle. Starting with the first answer, the second part of each answer carries down to become the first part of the following answer. With the clues given, complete the puzzle.

1. Inert _____
2. _____ _____
3. _____ _____
4. _____
5. _____
6. _____ _____
7. _____ roast

1. Neon or argon
2. It may be home on your range
3. Ebony
4. Vegas attraction
5. Type of dive
6. Cutter?
7. Butcher's offering

Petalgrams

Form six 7-letter words using the letters in each petal plus the F in the center. None of these words will begin with F. Then, form a 7-letter bonus word (beginning with F) using the first letter of each word you made plus the F.

Answers on page 178.

Split Decisions

Fill in each set of empty cells with letters that will create Scrabble words reading both across and down. Letters may repeat within a single set. We've completed one set to get you started.

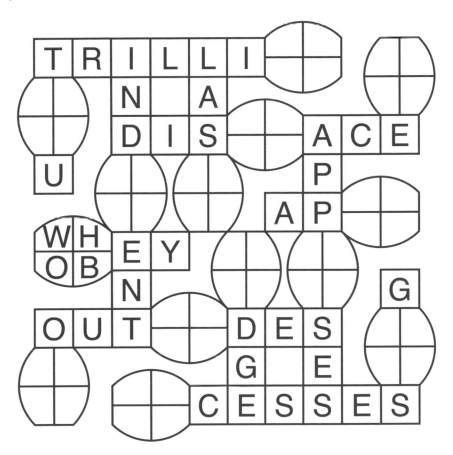

Each of the consonants in the phrase "KNIGHT SWIM" combines with -ae to form a valid play.

Answers on page 178.

Spin-o-Rama

Place the given words into the grid so they can be read around the spiral starting at the top left and traveling inwards. Words cannot overlap, and no row or column may contain the same letter more than once. We filled in one letter to get you started.

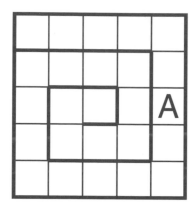

GAME

TRAPEZOID

GOAL   ZONE

SHOT

TERM

OPEN BOARD: When there are many places to play bingos or other high-scoring words.

Answers on page 179.

Bookend Letters

Each word below is missing a pair of identical letters. Add the same letter to the beginning and end of each word to create entirely new words. Do not use any pair of letters twice.

__ E A T __

__ E A R L __

__ E L U D E __

__ E V E __

__ E V O L V E __

Spin the Dials

Imagine that each of the dials below can spin. Turn each dial to form a 6-letter word reading straight across the middle of the 3 dials.

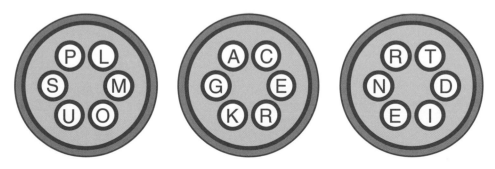

Answers on page 179.

SCRABBLE

Crossword Game

W₄ O₁ R₁ D₂

Inter-Textural

Each rack of seven letters below forms exactly one valid seven-letter bingo word. Unscramble them to find the bingo, then find words with six, five, four, three, and two letters each to complete the puzzle.

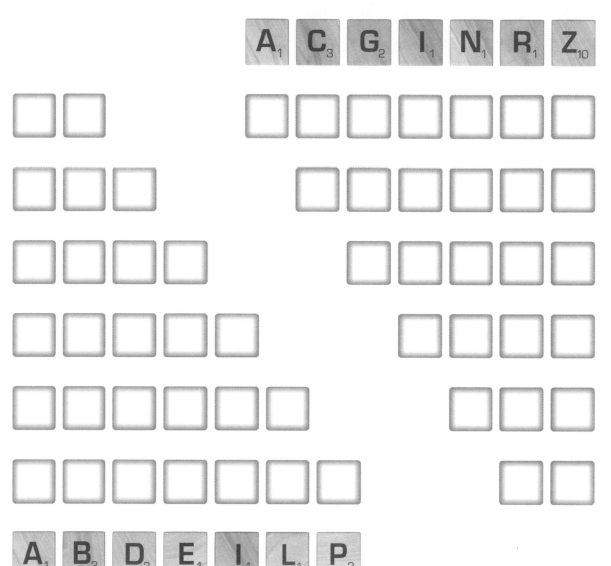

A₁ C₃ G₂ I₁ N₁ R₁ Z₁₀

A₁ B₃ D₂ E₁ I₁ L₁ P₃

Answers on page 179.

Words with Purpose

This puzzle works exactly like a crossword, only the clues are embedded within the grid. Arrows point to the direction the clue applies, either across or down.

Thick soup	▼	Resolute	Exceed-ingly	▼	Web-footed birds	Respect-able	▼	Saltwater fish	▼	Short tail
►				▼	Small cabin	►				
Notices		Heavy noble gas	►					Farm vehicle		Affirm-ative
►					Stylish	►		▼		▼
Small island		Repeat	►				Geologic time		Ring someone	
►				Burden	Garners	►	▼		▼	
Many times		Like a king	►		▼					After taxes
►					Rod	►				▼
Tactical man-cuvers		Quiet down	►				Unit	►		
►					White water bird	►				

COFFEE-HOUSING: To make small talk, crack knuckles, or do any of a number of things meant to distract or mislead your opponent.

SCRABBLE

W O R D

An Inward Spiral

This puzzle works exactly like a crossword, only without the divisions between words. In fact, some words blend into one another, so solving one clue will help you solve another. Numbers indicate the boxes answers occupy.

1	2	3	4	5	6	7	8	9
32	33	34	35	36	37	38	39	10
31	56	57	58	59	60	61	40	11
30	55	72	73	74	75	62	41	12
29	54	71	80		76	63	42	13
28	53	70	79	78	77	64	43	14
27	52	69	68	67	66	65	44	15
26	51	50	49	48	47	46	45	16
25	24	23	22	21	20	19	18	17

Answers on page 175.

1-5. Move slightly

1-6. Financial plan

5-10. Engraved deeply

7-13. Type of cheese

11-17. Superlatively black

14-20. Sparrow falcon

17-23. Latticework

21-26. Give heed to

24-29. Gentle and loving

27-32. Reason by deduction

29-34. Waterways

31-36. Parts of poems

35-42. Held in high regard

37-42. Swarmed

40-44. News sources

42-48. Using a rotary phone

45-50. Hang around

48-53. Rodent pet

51-58. Huge numbers

54-58. Predatory cats

56-60. Beginning

58-63. Breed of hunting dog

61-67. Most succinct

64-69. Group of six

67-72. Leash

70-74. Wading bird

73-76. A single time

75-80. Breakfast choice

77-80. Actual

Answers on page 179.

A Quick One, to Start

Use the clues to solve the puzzle. When complete, the circled letters will spell out a mystery word.

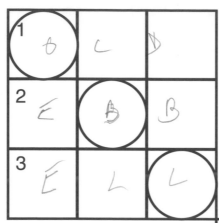

ACROSS
1. Aged
2. Tidal flow
3. Long, thin fish

DOWN
4. Irritate
5. Year count
6. Domesticated insect

Mystery word clue:
Make indebted

T₁ E₁ R₁ M₃

CLOSED BOARD: When there are few places to play bingos or other high-scoring words.

Answers on page 179.

Anagrammatically Correct

Fill in the blanks in each sentence below with 4-letter words that are anagrams (rearrangements of the same letters) of one another.

1. Use _____ baseball bat if you want to get more _____.

2. Male cats are called _____ by _____ people.

3. The man _____ his _____ hat on the bus.

4. The old man related his _____ until _____ in the evening.

5. An _____ of land was the prize promised to the winner of the _____.

6. My finger is still _____ where I pricked it on the thorn of a _____.

7. It rained _____ and dogs on the _____ during the last two _____ of the play when it was performed in the park.

8. It was a _____ to clean the pots and _____ while the kids were taking their _____.

An Obvious Answer

These seven letters spell exactly one valid seven-letter Scrabble word. Can you find it?

D E E V I N T

Answers on page 179.

SCRABBLE

W O R D

Word Web

It's a crossword without clues! Place the all professions into the grid to complete the puzzle. There's only one solution.

ACTOR
AGENT
ARTIST
BAKER
BUILDER
CLERK
COMIC
DENTIST
DOCTOR
JUDGE
MAYOR
MINER
MODEL
NURSE
PILOT
SINGER
SOLDIER
SURGEON
TEACHER
WRITER

Answers on page 179.

Word Jigsaw

Fit the pieces into the frame to form Scrabble words reading across and down.
There's no need to rotate the pieces; they'll fit as shown, with each piece used once.

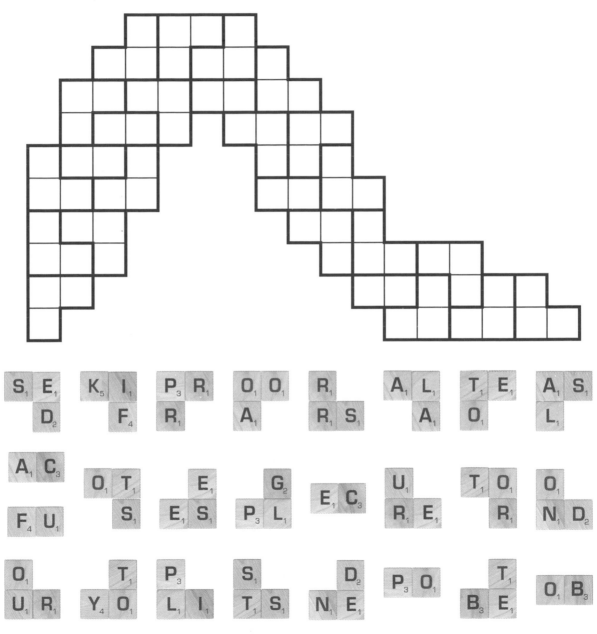

Word Ladder

Change just one letter on each line to go from the top word to the bottom word.
Do not change the order of the letters. You must have a Scrabble word at each step.

1. SNAP

_____
_____
_____
SHOT

3. LAKE

_____
_____
_____
_____
MEAD

5. ROSE

_____
_____
_____
_____
BUDS

2. MILK

_____
_____
_____
PAIL

4. SAIL

_____
_____
_____
_____
BOAT

Link Them

In the middle squares, place 3 letters that will complete one word and start another.
For example, TAR would complete GUI TAR GET.

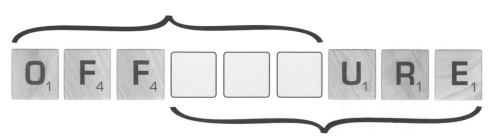

O₁ F₄ F₄ ☐ ☐ ☐ U₁ R₁ E₁

Answers on page 180.

Rhyme Time

Each clue leads to a 2-word answer that rhymes, such as BIG PIG or STABLE TABLE. The numbers in parentheses after the clue give the number of letters in each word.

1. **Plumbing problem (4, 4):** _____ _____

2. **Entrée option (4, 4):** _____ _____

3. **Go on a road trip (4, 4):** _____ _____

4. **Obsessive one's objective (4, 4):** _____ _____

5. **Bovine that just ate (4, 4):** _____ _____

6. **"Jack and Jill" (4, 4):** _____ _____

7. **Trumpeter's oldest instrument (4, 4):** _____ _____

8. **Base stealer's maneuver (4, 5):** _____ _____

9. **Spectral party giver (5, 4):** _____ _____

10. **The "and" after "Four score" (5, 4):** _____ _____

11. **Equine army (5, 5):** _____ _____

12. **Pronouncement by U.S. Customs (6, 5):** _____ _____

13. **More irate snake (6, 5):** _____ _____

14. **Writer's advance (6, 6):** _____ _____

15. **Stronger snub (6, 8):** _____ _____

Answers on page 180.

SCRABBLE

Crossword Game

W₄ O₁ R₁ D₂

Tangled Words

Think of this puzzle like a word search, only in reverse. Rather than finding the words in the grid, your job is to fill them in. Words begin only from the letters given in the shaded boxes and they appear in a straight line horizontally, vertically, or diagonally. They may appear forward or backward. When complete, every word will have been used, and the grid will have no empty squares.

ALPHABET	PLUNGE
ATOLLS	PRIVATE
BITTERSWEET	PROCREATE
CUPBOARD	PSALM
CYCLICAL	REFLEXES
EGRESSES	REPRINT
EMBASSY	RESTAURANT
ENVY	ROMPING
EXECUTE	SACRIFICE
EXPLORE	SALSA
FERAL	SCARCELY
FREAK	SEAR
GALLIVANT	SLUDGE
GALORE	SOME
GENES	STUMPS
GOING	TEMPT
JOLT	TRAMPLE
LINEAR	TRELLIS
PACED	UNSEEN
PERPETUAL	ZAPPED
PIETY	

The grid contains the following letters:

Row 1: A₁ · · · · S₁ · · · · · B₃ S₁
Row 2: · · · · · A₁ G₂ · · · · · R₁
Row 3: · · · Z₁₀ C P₃ · · · · E₁ ·
Row 4: · J₈ · · · R₁ · F₄ · · · ·
Row 5: · · · · · i · · · · S₁ · T₁
Row 6: · · · · f P₃ · C₃ · · · ·
Row 7: · · T₁ · P₃ i · · · · U₁
Row 8: R₁ E₁ · · · G · F₄ · · ·
Row 9: G₂ · · · e · P₃ · · P₃ ·
Row 10: E₁ · · · · · · · S₁ ·
Row 11: · · C₃ · · · · · · ·
Row 12: · L₁ · · · · · · · ·
Row 13: S₁ O M E G₂ D E L S₁ · · E₁

Answers on page 180.

Always look for plays parallel to words already on the SCRABBLE board. You get points for every word you form.

Addagram

This puzzle functions exactly like an anagram with an added step: In addition to being scrambled, each word below is missing the same letter. Discover the missing letter, then unscramble the words.

1. You'll reveal a poisonous element, a horticulturist, and words meaning "to wander" and "to foster."

C₃ A₁ S₁ E₁ I₁ N₁

B₃ L₁ A₁ M₃ E₁

D₂ E₁ R₁ A₁ N₁ G₂ E₁

U₁ N₁ T₁ R₁ U₁ E₁

2. You'll reveal an herb, a candy ingredient, a heavenly body, and somebody who is excluded.

O₁ R₁ A₁ N₁ G₂ E₁

D₂ A₁ S₁ T₁ I₁ E₁ R₁

G₂ A₁ U₁ N₁ T₁

T₁ I₁ R₁ U₁ D₂ E₁ S₁

Network

Place letters into the empty circles so that the given word can be spelled out in order from letter to consecutive letter through connected circles. Letters can be used more than once.

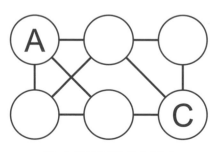

BARBECUE

Answers on page 180.

Avian Home

Travel in sequence through the puzzle from the left side to the right, using each numbered clue to determine the correct word. Connect adjacent words together with a common letter to proceed through the maze. Some letters are already given. The first and last words tie into the title.

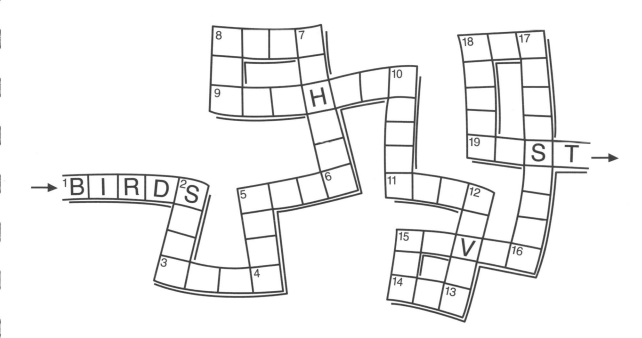

1. Feathered creatures
2. Categorize
3. Canvas dwelling
4. Slow run
5. Verbalize
6. Rabbi approved
7. Interpret writing
8. Patriarch
9. Debonair
10. Grind teeth
11. Chopped meat
12. Float
13. Fish eggs
14. Completion
15. Scuba _____
16. Guaranteed again
17. Form of tobacco
18. Not ornate
19. Stack together

Answers on page 180.

Pharmacy Fountain

Fill in the blank spaces as you would a crossword puzzle. The theme — or title — of the puzzle might appear to be ambiguous, but it should suggest a category of words that, when linked together, will complete the puzzle.

For example, HOLE IN ONE might suggest DOUGHNUTS. Or, it might suggest GOLF, which would lead to the words CLUB, IRON, TEE, etc. But all of these words have a common theme. Notice that a few letters are already in place, and some of the words intersect — adding to the mystery and the fun of finding the solution.

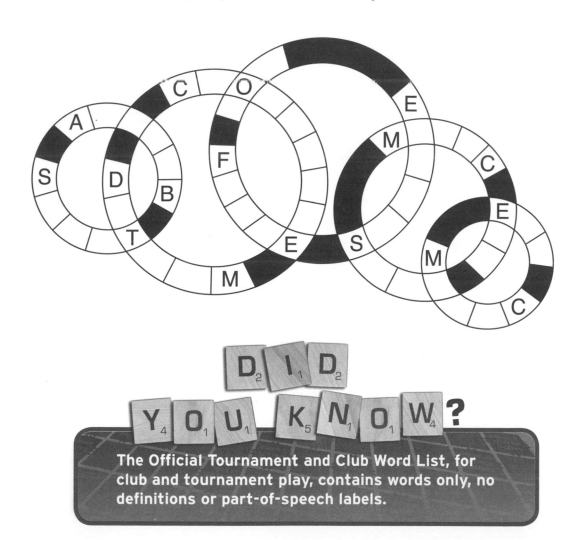

DID YOU KNOW?

The Official Tournament and Club Word List, for club and tournament play, contains words only, no definitions or part-of-speech labels.

Answers on page 180.

Pillers of Society

Each rack of seven letters below forms exactly one valid seven-letter bingo word. Unscramble them to find the bingo, then find words with six, five, four, three, and two letters each to complete the puzzle.

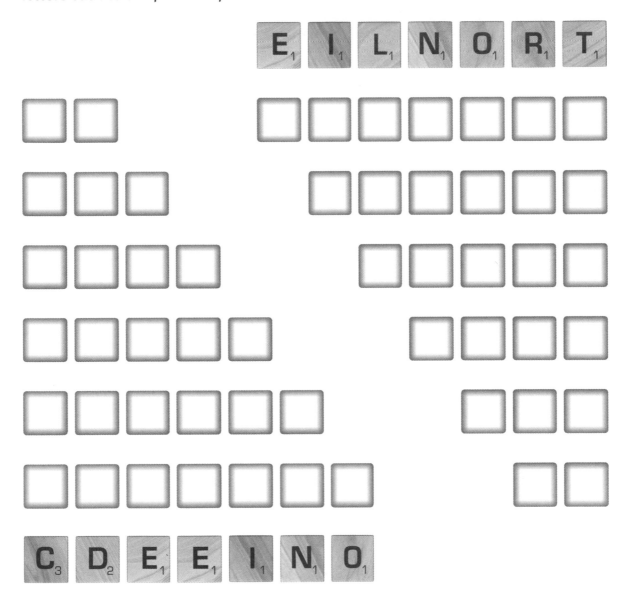

E I L N O R T

C D E E I N O

Animal Names

Cryptograms are messages in substitution code. Break the code to read the message. THE SMART CAT might become FVO QWGDF JGF if F is substituted for T, V for H, O for E, and so on. Look for repeated letters. E, T, A, O, N, R, and I are the most often used letters. The code is the same for each of these animal names.

1. TMDDQDQKCLNX
2. TCLXKVY
3. UMQJ
4. FMYCHHV
5. YCIIMK

6. LQNJKCMJ FQCK
7. VUVDTCJK
8. QDQXXNL
9. LQQXV
10. YTMJQOVYQX

Elevator Words

Like an elevator, words move up and down the "floors" of this puzzle. Starting with the first answer, the second part of each answer carries down to become the first part of the following answer. With the clues given, complete the puzzle.

1. Pitching _____
2. _____ _____
3. _____ _____
4. _____ _____
5. _____ _____
6. _____ _____
7. _____ to

1. It's used to loft golf balls over obstacles
2. Alternative for ladies shoes
3. Part of the tarsus
4. Fine porcelain
5. Where fine porcelain may be kept
6. Senior politician (UK)
7. Take care of

Answers on pages 180-181.

Word Ladder

Use the clues to change just one letter on each line to go from the top word to the bottom word. Do not change the order of the letters. You must have a Scrabble word at each step.

1. HALTER

_____ to waver

_____ having gained weight

_____ the substance

_____ the ruler

_____ speedier

_____ to secure

HASTEN

2. CRIME

_____ festering filth

_____ petty complaint

_____ dog food

_____ non-literal figure of speech

TROVE

Word Spiral

Find the 2 eight-letter words that are synonyms. One word reads clockwise around one square, the other reads counterclockwise around the other square. Find the starting points and add the missing letters.

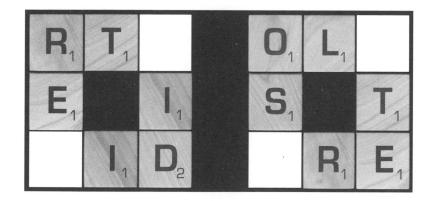

Answers on page 181.

Themeless

It's a crossword without clues! Place all the professions into the grid to complete the puzzle. There's only one solution.

3 LETTERS
CAR
CAT

4 LETTERS
BABY
BELL
BOAT
FISH
PLAY
ROSE
SHOE
SNOW

5 LETTERS
HORSE
HOUSE

6 LETTERS
FARMER
FATHER
FLOWER
MOTHER

8 LETTERS
AIRPLANE

DID YOU KNOW?

Like chess and bridge, competitive SCRABBLE gameplay is hugely popular and continues to add players every year.

Answers on page 181.

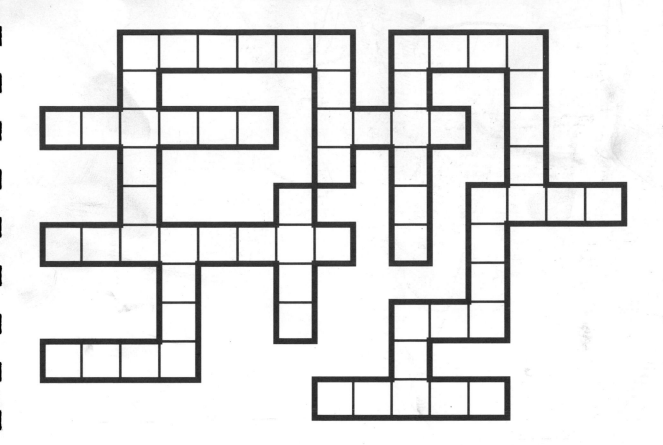

Letter Tiles

Using the letter tiles, create 5 five-letter words. Keep going. Can you create 10?

R A T I O N A L

Answers on page 181.

W₄ O₁ R₁ D₂

Family Function

Use the clues to solve the puzzle. When complete, the circled letters will spell out a mystery word.

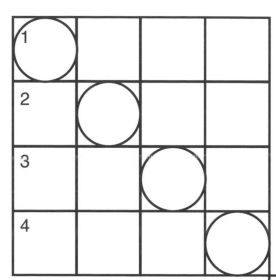

ACROSS
1. Not rich
2. Wide smile
3. Needle/yarn craft
4. Wet precipitation

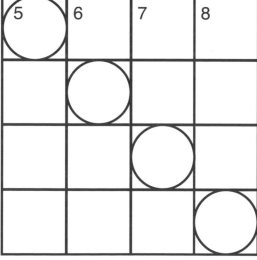

DOWN
5. Play actors group
6. 1/100 of $1
7. Stockings
8. Gluteus maximi

Mystery word clue:
Royal daughter

Answers on page 181.

Crypto-Wisdom

Cryptograms are messages in substitution code. Break the code to read the message. For example, THE SMART CAT might become FVO QWGDF JGF if F is substituted for T, V for H, O for E, and so on. Break the code to reveal the message. The code is different for each cryptogram.

1. FJCCM BL H DBLGLK JA OEK BDHNBIHOBJI.

2. HCB GDKIH HCLJM FEDAH PLIHFNBI LJ HCB NLHOCBJ LI HCFH RDA AIAFSSR CFTB HD BFH HCBP.

3. HB GBA IBDCLA AEFA FJJDLKMFAMBG MN FROFPN FJJDLKMFALH.

Mystery List

Larry just received an e-mail from his nephew Billy with the following wish list of presents for his sixth birthday.

FPH
NOLR
DLSYRNPSTF
YPU TPNPY

Clearly, something is wrong with this list. Can you help Larry determine what Billy really wants?

Answers on page 181.

E Pyramid

To build this pyramid, we begin by placing an **E** at the very top. To find the answer to each consecutive clue and fill in the remaining layers, add a letter to the previous answer as you move downward.

E

1. Masculine pronoun

2. Feminine pronoun

3. Storage building

4. Avoided

5. Protect

TRIPLE-TRIPLE: When a player makes a play that covers two Triple Word Squares. Multiply by nine the sum of the value of the letters of the "Triple-Triple" word.

Answers on page 181.

Divine Intervention

Each rack of seven letters below forms exactly one valid seven-letter bingo word. Unscramble them to find the bingo, then find words with six, five, four, three, and two letters each to complete the puzzle.

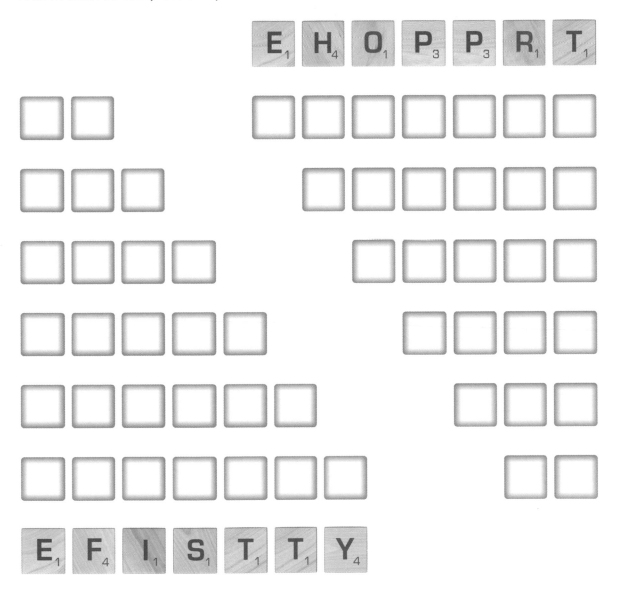

E H O P P R T

E F I S T T Y

Answers on page 181.

In the House?

Use the clues to solve the puzzle. When complete, the circled letters will spell out a mystery word.

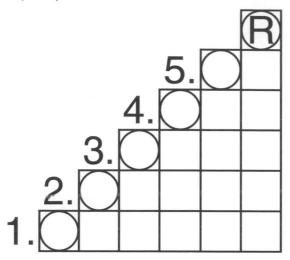

ACROSS

1. One losing weight
2. Prescription
3. Dieters avoid this
4. Hospital name label
5. "Using" a diet

Mystery word:

_____

A Wise Man Said It

Find the hidden phrase by using the letters directly below each of the blank squares. Each in a column letter is used only once in the squares above it.

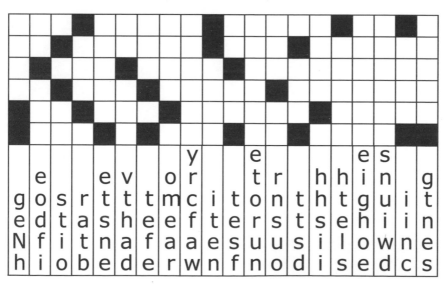

Answers on page 181.

Connections

This puzzle tests your ability to recognize common word roots. Each of the words below can stand on its own. However, each of these words can — with the addition of another word — be transformed into a compound word. Each series of words below shares the same root word. Your task is to find that root word. The root word can either precede or follow the given words. Hyphenated words are acceptable. For example: FLY MILK PEANUT (Answer: BUTTER).

1. HOOD   GRAND   STEP   _____

2. SAND   CAR   MAIL   _____

3. GROUND   HORSE   BONE   _____

4. CAT   LIFE   HOG   _____

5. WORM   STORY   MARK   _____

Sort and Fit

Fit the pieces into the frame to form Scrabble words reading across and down. There's no need to rotate the pieces; they'll fit as shown, with each piece used once.

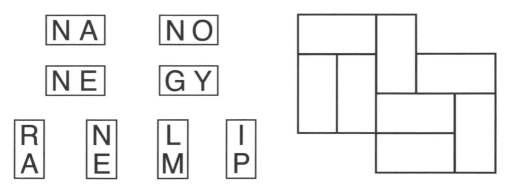

Answers on page 182.

The Loopy Lexicon

You probably won't find the clues for these 10 words in your typical dictionary. But they're a fun way of looking at words in a fresh and "logical" way. Or is that "psycho"-logical?

Across

1. Insect that lives on castaways?

4. Boat just for guys?

7. Thug with a babe?

8. Wacky way to move?

9. Light rain in Italy?

10. Baby talk?

Down

2. Unisex wedding attendant?

3. Less hairy race?

5. Dance tunes for lumberjacks?

6. Prison seminar?

The words:

BALDERDASH

BIGAMIST

BRIDEGROOM

CONCOURSE

FATHERHOOD

FELLOWSHIP

LITTERBUG

LOCOMOTION

LOGARITHMS

PREDICTION

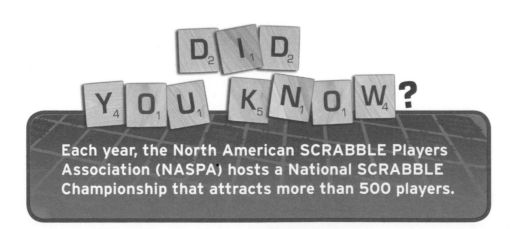

DID YOU KNOW?

Each year, the North American SCRABBLE Players Association (NASPA) hosts a National SCRABBLE Championship that attracts more than 500 players.

Another Word for It

You are given 2 words. Your objective is to come up with a set of homophones (words that sound alike but are spelled differently) that would either precede or follow each of these words. For example, GUITAR and SECOND would be BASS and BASE.

TENNIS, NUMBERS

Answers on page 182.

W O R D

Pop the Question

Each rack of seven letters below forms exactly one valid seven-letter bingo word. Unscramble them to find the bingo, then find words with six, five, four, three, and two letters each to complete the puzzle.

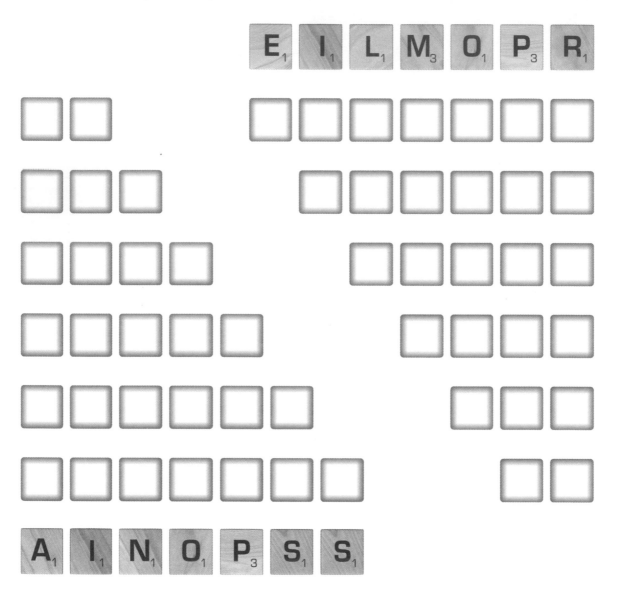

E I L M O P R

A I N O P S S

Answers on page 182.

Rhyme Time

Each clue leads to a 2-word answer that rhymes, such as BIG PIG or STABLE TABLE. The numbers in parentheses after the clue give the number of letters in each word.

1. Captive's plea (4, 2): _____ _____
2. Bargain in the citrus section (4, 4): _____ _____
3. Mailed a large monthly payment (4, 4): _____ _____
4. Remains agreeable (5, 4): _____ _____
5. Sign just before the turn (5, 4): _____ _____
6. Excel at the bee (5, 4): _____ _____
7. Trapper's backup (5, 5): _____ _____
8. Restocking shelves, e.g. (5, 5): _____ _____
9. Especially commonplace (5, 5): _____ _____
10. Run-of-the-mill prom (6, 6): _____ _____

Makes a Good Dog

Unscramble the letters in each line to solve the puzzle. The words cross on a letter that they share.

```
        H
        C
        K
        P
        E
T U A D S R M
        T
```

It's All Behind You

Use the clues to solve the puzzle. When complete, the circled letters will spell out a mystery word.

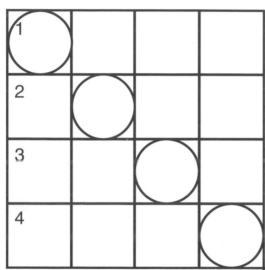

ACROSS
1. Bleed (past tense)
2. Say (past tense)
3. Decorative edging
4. Storage display

DOWN
5. Sleigh
6. Spherical adornment
7. A type of moss
8. Precise

Mystery word hint:
Rear position

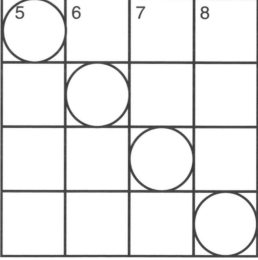

Answers on page 182.

Word Ladder

Change just one letter on each line to go from the top word to the bottom word.
Do not change the order of the letters. You must have a Scrabble word at each step.

1. ROCK

——

——

——

MICE

3. SOCK

——

——

——

BOOT

2. YARD

——

——

——

DIRT

4. PARK

——

——

——

CORN

FISHING: To play only one or two tiles, keeping five or six really good tiles, with the hope of playing a high-scoring word next turn.

Add-a-Letter

This is a standard word search with a twist: For each word in the list, you must add one letter to form a new word, which you will then search for in the grid. For example: If the listed word is CARTON, you'd search for CARTOON; if the listed word is OTTER, you might have to search for HOTTER or POTTER. The words can be found in a straight line horizontally, vertically, or diagonally, and may read forward or backward.

ARSON

BASTED

BEAT

BOUGHT

FAIL

FAKED

FORTH

HALER

HERON

LENT

MASH

NAVES

REALLY

REPEL

RESENT

RUBLE

RUSED

SEEK

SEER

SINK

SPIT

TALE

TINE

TUMBLE

YAWING

```
S B D Q M S Y W B C R Q J
R L W A P L L P L E N T O
A A R R L R B E L C F C O
S S I A O D E U E O E E B
H T G K B T A S U K L O T
B E U X N H S R E B B B D
R D R M I I T D B N A E F
O E S O B H T U P O T K T
U B P E I L R S L S O A H
G O G E I N E I U R Q L F
H U V E A V A R T A Z F L
T H I N E L A B Y P R V I
H A M R F D G N I N W A Y
```

Balanced Letters

Many letters are symmetrical on their vertical or horizontal axis. Some letters, such as H, I, O, and X are symmetrical on both axes. Of the letter pairs below, which have a horizontal symmetry?

1. L, Z
2. W, Y
3. D, E
4. F, M

Letter Sets

The letters below are arranged into 3 groups based on a design reason. Which group should the letter H belong to?

A. L T V
B. A K N
C. E M W

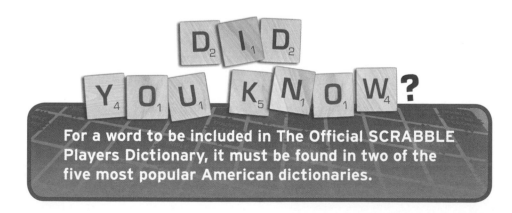

DID YOU KNOW?

For a word to be included in The Official SCRABBLE Players Dictionary, it must be found in two of the five most popular American dictionaries.

Answers on page 182.

Honeycomb Cross

Answer each clue with a 6-letter word. Write the words in a clockwise direction around the numbers in the grid. Words overlap each other and may start in any of the spaces around the numerals. We've placed some letters to get you started.

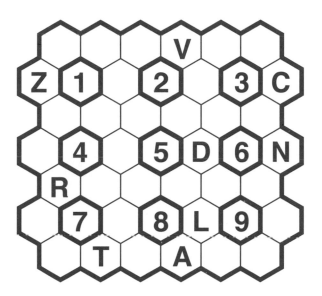

1. Electric signaling device
2. Obtain
3. Repeat performance
4. Eraser material
5. Coated with color
6. Talked monotonously
7. Attractive
8. Real
9. Refusal to agree

What Castles Are Made Of

A series of different letters have been tacked on to the word CASTLE. Make new words by rearranging the letters, with a little help from the hints.

1. CASTLE + H = _____ Hint: Alpine homes

2. CASTLE + I = _____ Hint: Stretchy

3. CASTLE + M = _____ Hint: Least ruffled

4. CASTLE + K = _____ Hint: Football linemen

5. CASTLE + R = _____ Hint: Bright red

Answers on pages 182-183.

Words to Wave At

Fill in each white square with a different letter so a trio of related words is formed.

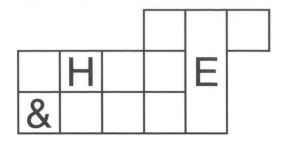

Keep It Flowing

Spell a 10-letter word by moving between adjacent letters. Every letter will be used at least once, but no letter will be used consecutively. Begin at any letter.

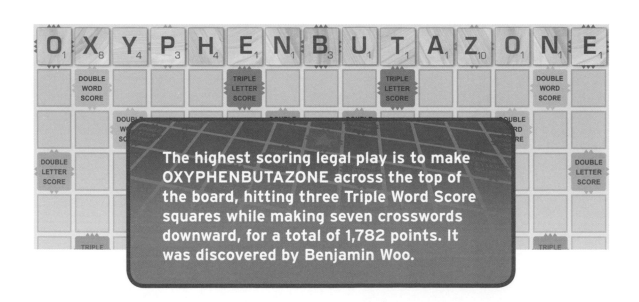

The highest scoring legal play is to make OXYPHENBUTAZONE across the top of the board, hitting three Triple Word Score squares while making seven crosswords downward, for a total of 1,782 points. It was discovered by Benjamin Woo.

Answers on page 183.

Double Them Up

This puzzle works exactly like a crossword, except instead of placing one letter in each box, you place two. Words are written across in each box. As a bonus, unscramble the letters found in the shaded boxes to answer the definition below.

ACROSS

1. Territory, region

5. Cave in

6. Solitary

8. Unfastens

10. Funny man

11. From the East

DOWN

2. Conquer

3. Look into

4. Earmark

7. Eventually

8. Bearing

9. Of marriage

Ordinary: _____

Try to reserve the blanks for 40-50+ point plays.

Answers on page 183.

Tour de Force

Each rack of seven letters below forms exactly one valid seven-letter bingo word. Unscramble them to find the bingo, then find words with six, five, four, three, and two letters each to complete the puzzle.

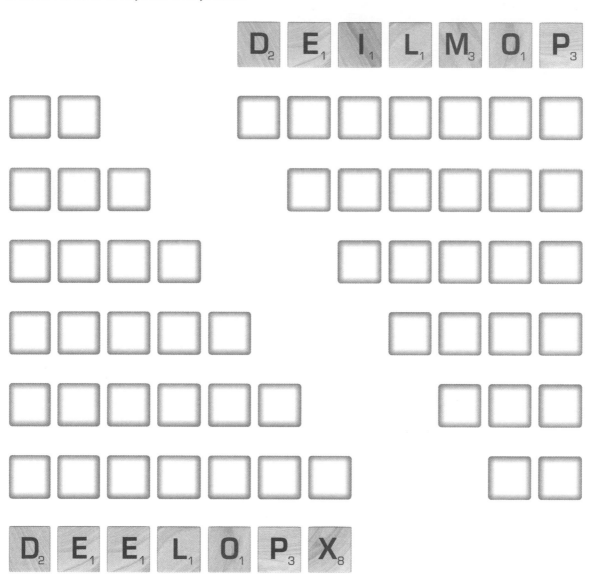

Geography Scrambler

Four 11-letter words, all of which revolve around the same theme, have been jumbled. Unscramble each word, and write the answer in the accompanying space. Next, transfer the letters in the shaded boxes into the shaded keyword space, and unscramble the 9-letter word that goes with the theme. The theme for this puzzle is geography.

Double Rhyme

Each clue leads to a 2- or 3-word answer that rhymes, such as BIG PIG or STABLE TABLE. The numbers in parentheses after the clue give the number of letters in each word. For example, "cookware taken from the oven (3, 3)" would be HOT POT.

1. Large fruit from a woody New Testament plant (3,3) _____ _____

2. Why the fruit was a surprise (3,4) _____ _____

3. Outer garment made from a sheep cousin (4,4) _____ _____

4. Reliable information from a New Testament book (4,5) _____ _____

5. One thing that Abel did (4,5) _____ _____

6. Error in choice of psalms (5,4) _____ _____

7. Moses' effort to get the waters to part (3,3,4) _____ _____ _____

Wedge Words

Fit the words into the grid reading across and down. Each word is used once.

BEAD   OVER

ENDS   PEAR

ERRS   ROBE

OVEN   ROPE

Answers on page 183.

2 Rules

Cryptograms are messages in substitution code. Break the code to read the message. For example, THE SMART CAT might be FVO QWGDF JGF if F is substituted for T, V for H, O for E, and so on.

Hint: Look for repeated letters. E, T, A, O, N, R, and I are the most-often-used letters. A single letter is usually A or I; OF, IS, and IT are common 2-letter words; THE and AND are common 3-letter groups.

> HNMFM TFM HIG FPQMK WGF PQHCJTHM KPAAMKK CO
> QCWM. OMSMF HMQQ MSMFLHNCOY LGP EOGI.

A Challenging Thing to Do

Find the hidden phrase by using the letters directly below each of the blanks in the grid. Each letter is used only once. A black square or the end of the line indicates the end of a word.

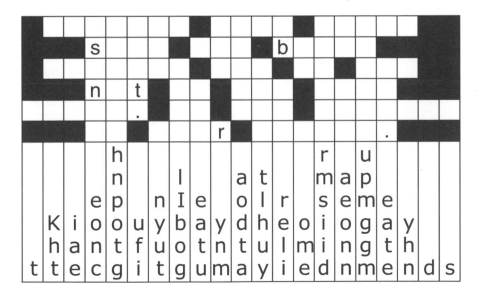

SCRABBLE

Crossword Game

W₄ O₁ R₁ D₂

A Happy Holiday

It's 2 jumbles in one! First, unscramble the 7 letters under each row of squares to form Scrabble words. When you've done this, unscramble the letters running down each column in the blackened boxes to reveal 2 more words.

L S F E O E N

E A G S S U O

S L K S E Y E

B L I E N G O

F R S I F E H

E C L G T E N

U B T A E L A

E R I B L C A

T₁ E₁ R₁ M₃

NATURAL BINGO: A bingo that does not use a blank tile.

Answers on page 183.

Decorations

Plug in the appropriate 7 consonants to find the word.

O A E A I O

Grid Fill

To complete this puzzle, place the given letters and words into the shapes in this grid. Words and letters will run across, down, and wrap around each shape. When the grid is filled, each row will contain one of the following words: Bolts, Fools, Liars, Spoon, Stamp, Tawas

1. O, S
2. AT, SS
3. OWL
4. FOOT, LAMP, SLIP, STAB
5. ARSON

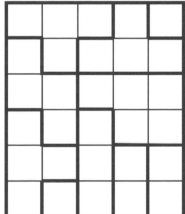

OVERDRAWING: When one player draws more tiles from the bag than is appropriate.

Answers on pages 183-184.

Got Hot

Each clue leads to a 2-word answer that rhymes, such as BIG PIG or STABLE TABLE. The numbers in parentheses after the clue give the number of letters in each word. For example, "cookware taken from the oven (3, 3)" would be HOT POT.

1. Became overheated (3, 3): _____ _____

2. Rudely ignore baby bear (3, 4): _____ _____

3. Sluggish river current (4, 4): _____ _____

4. College housing application (4, 4): _____ _____

5. More elegant cruise ship (5, 5): _____ _____

6. Earthquake cause (4, 5): _____ _____

7. Reading room with tracked-in muck (5, 5): _____ _____

8. Arrive at sandy expanse (5, 5): _____ _____

9. Unpleasant surprise from a market decline (5, 5): _____ _____

10. Majestic raptor (5, 5): _____ _____

Word Circle

Complete each 6-letter word so the last 2 letters of the first word are the first 2 letters of the second word, and the last 2 letters of the second word are the first 2 letters of the third word, etc. The last 2 letters of the final word are the first 2 letters of the first word, thus completing the circle.

```
_ _ L L _ R          _ _ E V E _
_ _ O U _ _          _ _ T I _ _
_ _ Q U _ _
```

Answers on page 184.

Cast-a-Word

There are 4 dice, and there are different letters of the alphabet on the 6 faces of each of them (each letter appears only once). Random throws of the dice produced the words in this list. Can you figure out which letters appear on each of the 4 dice?

BORN	**MOPE**
DOLT	**POKY**
DONE	**TUBE**
FACE	**TUCK**
FISH	**VIEW**
GARB	**WAXY**
IRON	**WHIP**
JACK	

Bird Words

Each horizontal row and vertical column contains the name of a bird. Find all 18 birds by circling the correct letters in each row and column. All letters in the grid are used only once.

J	H	E	O	A	G	D	L	E
E	O	D	M	P	T	U	H	L
R	R	O	W	H	O	U	A	K
S	N	W	A	E	I	C	N	A
F	L	A	M	A	I	N	G	O
H	B	O	E	S	N	K	W	R
A	I	C	L	A	R	O	K	W
G	L	V	U	N	T	L	L	K
Y	L	E	H	T	E	R	O	N

Add-a-Letter

This is a standard word search with a twist: For each word in the list, you must add one letter to form a new word, which you will then search for in the grid. For example: If the listed word is CARTON, you'd search for CARTOON; if the listed word is OTTER, you might have to search for HOTTER or POTTER. The words can be found in a straight line horizontally, vertically, or diagonally, and may read forward or backward.

ADDLE	PARK
CLOSET	PITY
CRACKED	PONY
DEBT	REVEL
DRAWING	ROUE
DRIER	ROUND
FATHER	SABLE
GALLON	SANK
GASSY	SCARE
GRATER	SICKER
HARMED	SOLDER
HATH	SORT
HEIRS	SOUR
HERO	STAY
HUNTED	STEW
LATITUDE	THROUGH
OUNCE	WORD

```
S W M R H S D S O L D I E R R
S K D V E K T E T U X E C R E
T S P I T H Y A T R N O R E H
I S T R A Y T D B N O M A V T
N T D R X Y S A L L U N C E R
K H E E E D T S E R E A S A A
E O L L B W L N A F O U H L F
R R K D R I V E R R O W G Q K
F O C D R E T A E R G N I N R
E U U U J D E L K C I P A D E
K G H M P R B T W L S P A R K
V H C H T A E H W V S P X U C
G R O U N D G A L L E O N O I
I N G E P P R T H E I R S C N
Y E T P Q D X P O U N C E S S
```

W₄ O₁ R₁ D₂

Shooting Star

Continue to fill in the alphabet moving clockwise around the wheel. Put one letter in every third space until you fill in the whole wheel. Use all 26 letters of the alphabet. Then unscramble the 5 letters at the 5 points of the star to form a common 5-letter word.

All Kinds of People

These seven letters spell exactly one valid seven-letter Scrabble word. Can you find it?

D₂ H₄ I₁ I₁ M₃ N₁ O₁

Answers on page 184.

Goal in Mind

Use the clues to solve the puzzle. When complete, the circled letters will spell out a mystery word.

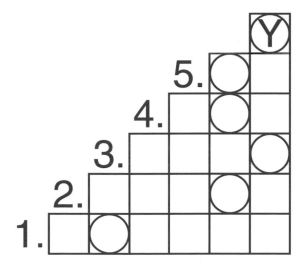

ACROSS
1. Netminder
2. Slapshot piece
3. Game missile
4. Goal location
5. Hello!

Mystery word hint:
Sport played on ice

Network

Enter letters into the empty circles so that the given word can be spelled out in order from letter to consecutive letter through connected circles. Letters can be used more than once.

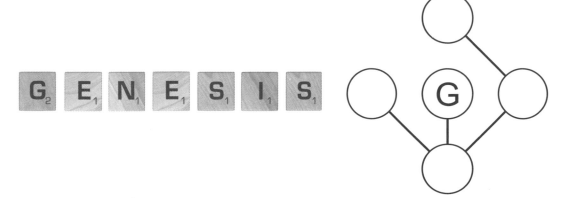

Answers on page 184.

Precious Little

Each rack of seven letters below forms exactly one valid seven-letter bingo word. Unscramble them to find the bingo, then find words with six, five, four, three, and two letters each to complete the puzzle.

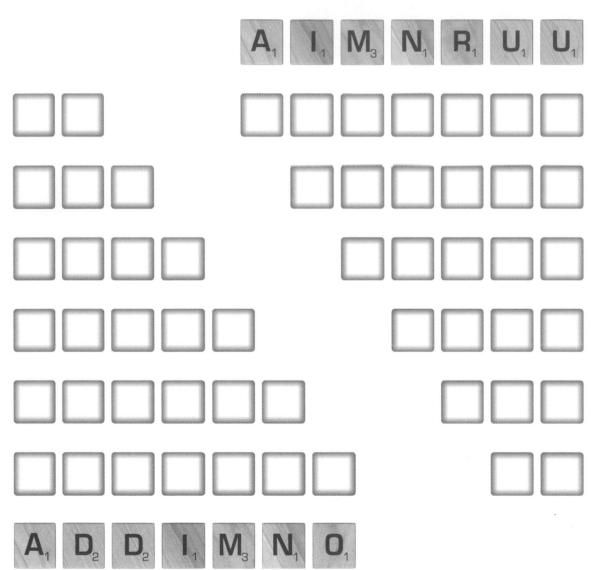

A I M N R U U

A D D I M N O

What to Do?

Follow the arrows to solve each clue and complete the grid.

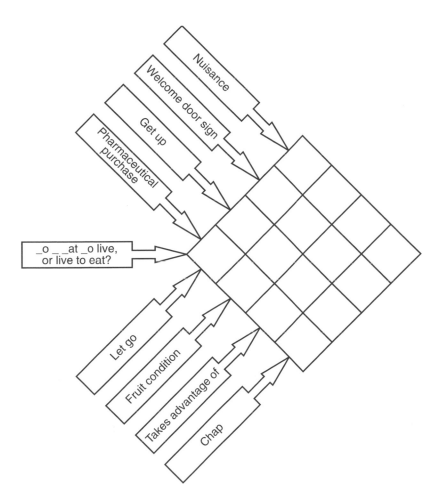

Brown Words

Use every letter of the phrase AN ALERT BRUTE WHALE (only once) to spell 3 things associated with the color brown.

Answers on pages 184-185.

SCRABBLE

W O R D

Acrostic Anagram

Unscramble the words below, then transfer the corresponding letters to the grid. The end of a word is signified by a black square. When you're finished, you'll be rewarded with a quote from Will Rogers.

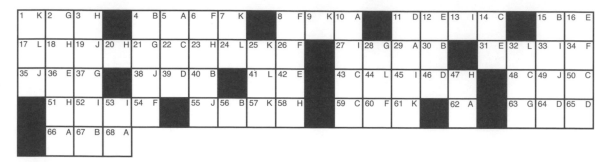

1 K	2 G	3 H	■	4 B	5 A	6 F	7 K	■	8 F	9 K	10 A	■	11 D	12 E	13 I	14 C	■	15 B	16 E
17 L	18 H	19 J	20 H	21 G	22 C	23 H	24 L	25 K	26 F	■	27 I	28 G	29 A	30 B	■	31 E	32 L	33 I	34 F
35 J	36 E	37 G	■	38 J	39 D	40 B	■	41 L	42 E	■	43 C	44 L	45 I	46 D	47 H	■	48 C	49 J	50 C
■	51 H	52 I	53 I	54 F	■	55 J	56 B	57 K	58 H	■	59 C	60 F	61 K	■	62 A	■	63 G	64 D	65 D
■	66 A	67 B	68 A																

A. Y A Y N W A

$\overline{62}\ \overline{29}\ \overline{68}\ \overline{66}\ \overline{5}\ \overline{10}$

B. T C R I A C

$\overline{67}\ \overline{40}\ \overline{4}\ \overline{30}\ \overline{56}\ \overline{15}$

C. Y W T E A R

$\overline{48}\ \overline{22}\ \overline{14}\ \overline{43}\ \overline{50}\ \overline{59}$

D. E W R T O

$\overline{11}\ \overline{39}\ \overline{65}\ \overline{53}\ \overline{46}$

E. I C A N H

$\overline{36}\ \overline{12}\ \overline{31}\ \overline{16}\ \overline{42}$

F. N Y A N S O

$\overline{34}\ \overline{6}\ \overline{26}\ \overline{60}\ \overline{54}\ \overline{8}$

G. Z O E O N

$\overline{28}\ \overline{21}\ \overline{2}\ \overline{63}\ \overline{37}$

H. Y I U T I L T

$\overline{3}\ \overline{23}\ \overline{18}\ \overline{58}\ \overline{20}\ \overline{51}\ \overline{47}$

I. E D H A E V

$\overline{52}\ \overline{64}\ \overline{13}\ \overline{33}\ \overline{45}\ \overline{27}$

J. A N K L F

$\overline{38}\ \overline{19}\ \overline{49}\ \overline{35}\ \overline{55}$

K. U O A Y T L

$\overline{57}\ \overline{9}\ \overline{1}\ \overline{25}\ \overline{61}\ \overline{7}$

L. D I V V I

$\overline{44}\ \overline{41}\ \overline{17}\ \overline{24}\ \overline{32}$

You Own It!

Spell a 10-letter word by moving between adjacent letters. Every letter will be used at least once, but no letter will be used consecutively. Begin at any letter.

Answers on page 185.

Word Ladder

Change just one letter on each line to go from the top word to the bottom word.
Do not change the order of the letters. You must have a Scrabble word at each step.

1. BANK

___

___

SAVE

2. BIRD

___

___

___

___

NEST

3. EARN

___

___

___

CASH

4. WINS

___

___

___

VOTE

Broken Word Chain

Place 3 letters in the middle squares that will complete one word and start another.
For example, TAR would complete GUI TAR GET.

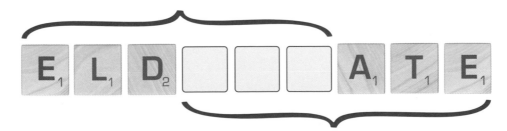

Answers on page 185.

Word Paths

Each of these word paths contains a familiar saying. To figure out the saying, read freely from letter to letter, starting with the letter indicated by the arrow. Some letters will be used more than once, and you can move forward and backward along the straight lines. The blanks indicate the number of letters in each word of the saying.

1.

2.

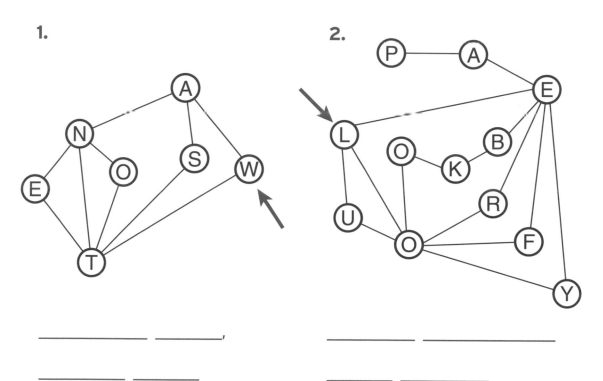

_____ _____,   _____ _____

_____ _____   _____ _____

T₁ I₁ P₃

Leave as few high-point tiles in your rack as possible.

Answers on page 185.

Tough Stuff

Each clue leads to a 2-word answer that rhymes, such as BIG PIG or STABLE TABLE. The numbers in parentheses after the clue give the number of letters in each word. For example, "cookware taken from the oven (3, 3)" would be HOT POT.

1. No charge Earl Grey (4,3): _____ _____

2. Hubby's response to wife's request to pick a beverage (4,4): _____ _____

3. He did the dishes, drove the kids, did the laundry, etc. upon request; he was a (5,4): _____ _____

4. Put on a sheer silk dress (3,7): _____ _____

5. Purse pun (7,3): _____ _____

6. She was very partial to a fine-grained leather (8,3): _____ _____

7. What was served at the monthly book get-together (4,4): _____ _____

8. A more expensive makeup (5,8): _____ _____

9. Poser about a cooking utensil (7,6): _____ _____

10. Encourages the ladies to dress for the hot weather (7,6): _____ _____

11. Where she kept certain jewelry (8,5): _____ _____

12. Dedicated to used of face cream (6,8): _____ _____

13. Part of a NYC vacation (8,4): _____ _____

Writer's Block

In the grid below is a scrambled, 16-letter word. Can you unscramble it to reveal the correct word?

U	T	L	O
I	G	R	H
C	A	I	A
B	O	A	P

Conflicting Traits

SECURE RACKS FELL is an anagram of which 2 words that are opposite in meaning?

Spin-o-Rama

Place the given words into the grid so they can be read around the spiral starting at the top left and traveling inward. Words cannot overlap, and no row or column may contain the same letter more than once.

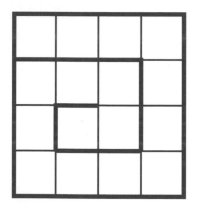

Word Circle

Complete the 6-letter words so that the last 2 letters of the first word are the first 2 letters of the second word, and the last 2 letters of the second word are the first 2 letters of the third word, and so on. The last 2 letters of the final word in the list are the first 2 letters of the first word, thus completing the circle.

__ __	**NP**	__ __
__ __	**VA**	__ __
__ __	**RI**	__ __
__ __	**RB**	__ __
__ __	**MO**	__ __
__ __	**UP**	__ __
__ __	**NA**	__ __

Answers on page 185.

Addagram

This puzzle functions exactly like an anagram with an added step: In addition to being scrambled, each word below is missing the same letter. Discover the missing letter, then unscramble the words.

1. You'll reveal a goal, a period of time, a place where performances are staged, and a word meaning "affluence."

GREAT   REHEAT

FROTHING   WHALE

2. You'll reveal a type of food baked in a deep dish, as well as words meaning "indignation," "to lessen," and "second-rate."

LACROSSE   CRUDE

RAGOUT   DORMICE

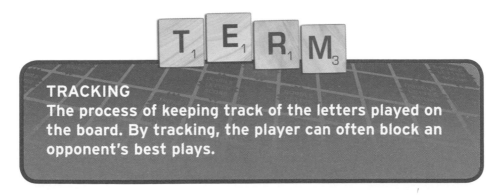

TERM

TRACKING
The process of keeping track of the letters played on the board. By tracking, the player can often block an opponent's best plays.

Answers on page 185.

Full of Science

Solve this puzzle just as you would a sudoku. Use deductive logic to complete the grid so that each row, column, and 3 by 3 box contains the letters from the word CHEMISTRY.

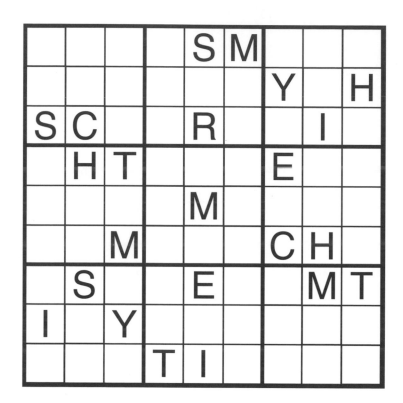

Can You Relate to This?

What is the longest word in the English language that can be produced from the letters **M E T K J P A B H Y**? No letter may be used more than once. Some letters may not be used.

Answers on page 185.

Timing Is Everything

Enter every letter of the alphabet into the grid. Letters are connected horizontally, vertically, or diagonally from A to Z. Use the clue to fill in the circles and help complete the grid.

Clue: Between day and night

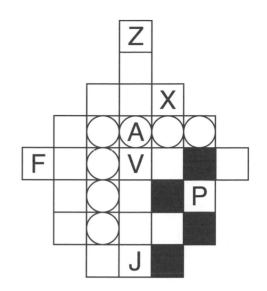

Same Old Thing!

Spell a 10-letter word by moving between adjacent letters. Every letter will be used at least once, but no letter will be used consecutively. Begin at any letter.

A Little Woolly

These seven letters spell exactly one valid seven-letter Scrabble word. Can you find it?

Answers on pages 185-186.

SCRABBLE

Get There Safely

Use the clues to solve the puzzle. When complete, the circled letters will spell out a mystery word.

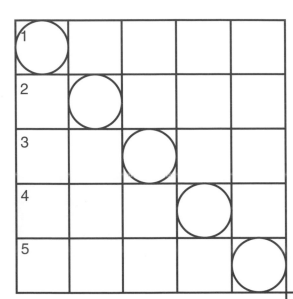

ACROSS
1. Surface mark
2. Lifting equipment
3. Whole milk component
4. Sandy water edge
5. Russian villa

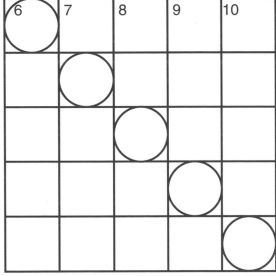

DOWN
6. Remove fastening
7. Map collection
8. Carry
9. Thin mattress
10. Fake

Mystery word clue:
Protective action

Answers on page 186.

Word Ladder

Change just one letter on each line to go from the top word to the bottom word.
Do not change the order of the letters. You must have a Scrabble word at each step.

1. GOOD

____

____

____

WILL

2. JELLY

____

____

____

BEANS

3. BIRD

____

____

____

CAGE

4. DUCKS

____

____

KINGS

DID YOU KNOW?

At SCRABBLE clubs and tournaments, experts average between 330-450 points per game.

Answers on page 186.

Add-a-Letter

This is a standard word search with a twist: For each word in the list, you must add one letter to form a new word, which you will then search for in the grid. For example: If the listed word is CARTON, you'd search for CARTOON; if the listed word is OTTER, you might have to search for HOTTER or POTTER. The words can be found in a straight line horizontally, vertically, or diagonally, and may read forward or backward.

BOON	PONY
BURRO	POSER
CANE	RAID
CAPER	RELAY
CAST	RESIDE
CHAR	RETAIN
CINCH	SCAPE
CLEVER	SERF
COOKED	SHANK
COUP	SICK
CURLED	SMOTHER
EXERT	SORE
FINER	SORT
FLING	STUDY
FORCES	TAPED
LATHER	UNCTION
PARTY	VIAL

```
Y T P U S T T B U X C O U P E
F D N E M H C R O O K E D C S
B U R R O W L R E R E X U O L
R F M U O N I P V P O B R A I
A C C Y T A Y A I W X N E S C
P U R B H S T R T Y S E P T K
I R E C E Z G T A K V N M X U
D D V R R N X L L N C A A S H
D L A H I Q P Y O X G R C C E
T E E Y D E R I T K F C N R R
A D L A R E T R A I N I P A O
P F C O T C O U N I L A V P H
P W K S N H P G A C F I R E S
E P O U S R E S I D U E F H Q
D P J R K R H R F O R C E P S
```

A Word to the Wise

In the lines below, cross out 12 letters in such a way that the remaining letters spell a Scrabble word.

Word Jumble

Create the shortest possible word in the English language using letters from the 3 words below.

Hint: The letter combinations MAR, AM, and FAR would produce the word FARM.

Wedge Words

Fit the words into the grid reading across and down. Each word is used once.
Two letters have been given to get you started.

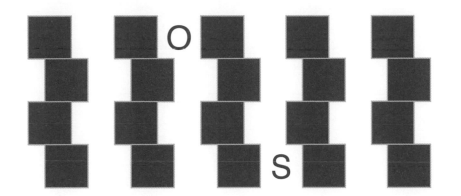

AREA
CAPE
COME
EASE
ELSE
MESS
ORAL
PASS

Perfect Fit

Fit the given words into the crossword grid. Be careful with your selections though –
more words are provided than are needed.

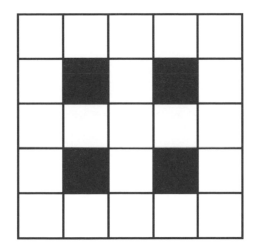

ALERT
BEGIN
BRAID
DITCH
FATED
GREAT
NOTCH
QUIRK

Answers on page 186.

SCRABBLE

Crossword Game

W₄ O₁ R₁ D₂

Follow the Arrows

This puzzle works exactly like a crossword, only the clues are embedded within the grid. Arrows point to the direction the clue applies, either across or down.

		Sports enthus-iast ▼	Focus of an earth-quake		▼	Doctrine		Ancient boat ▼		Talent	Killed
Later						Regula-tions ▶					▼
▶											
Bitterly pungent		Mountain top ▶						One		Guard	
▶						Cheat	Helper ▶	▼		▼	
Loung-ing wear		First light of day ▶				▼					
▶				Exclam-ation of dismay		Every		Com-puter virus ▼		Sweet potatoes ▼	
Voice part		Nothing ▶		▼		▼	Lopsided ▶	▼			
▶						Smell ▶					
Workers		Poem ▶						Male sheep ▶			
▶				Songs of praise ▶							

To the Letter

Fill in the blanks with words that are nearly identical to each other. Figure out the first word, then drop one letter to discover the second word. Do not rearrange the letters.

Having my own private _____ is my _____, should I ever win the lotto.

Answers on page 186.

Fashionable Scramblegram

Four 8-letter words, all of which revolve around the same theme, have been jumbled. Unscramble each word, and write the answer in the accompanying space. Next, transfer the letters in the shaded boxes into the shaded keyword spaces, and unscramble the 9-letter word that goes with the theme. The theme for this puzzle is clothing.

Over and Oat

Each rack of seven letters below forms exactly one valid seven-letter bingo word.
Unscramble them to find the bingo, then find words with six, five, four, three, and two
letters each to complete the puzzle.

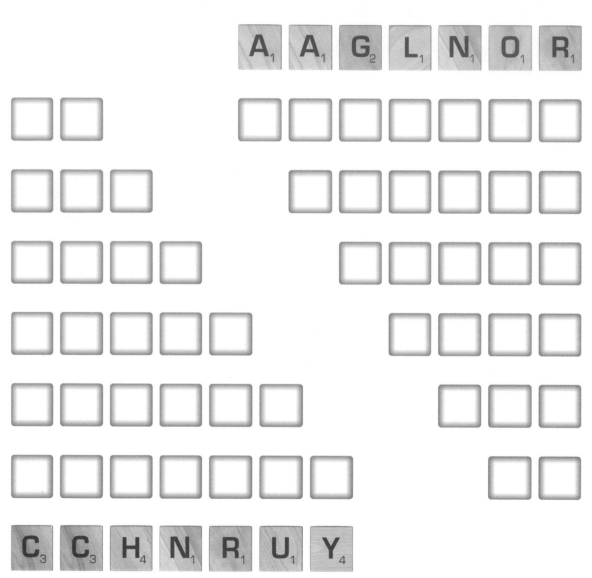

6-Letter Anagrams

Fill in the blanks in each sentence below with 6-letter words that are anagrams (rearrangements of the same letters) of one another.

1. The athlete who _____ too hard may _____ some of her muscles.

2. Those who _____ to greatness are often merely after the _____ and adulation of their peers.

3. It is a _____ feeling to know that a lifeguard will _____ you if you get into trouble while swimming.

4. When the sightseeing group _____ the south of France they came to a road under construction and had to _____ from their route.

5. My _____ and I could never _____ building a snowman in the winter.

6. I hate close work so my _____ for sewing begins when I _____ the needle.

Take the Elevator

Like an elevator, words move up and down the "floors" of this puzzle. Starting with the first answer, the second part of each answer carries down to become the first part of the following answer. With the clues given, complete the puzzle.

1. Potato _____   1. Burger side

2. _____ _____   2. Romaine, for one

3. _____ _____   3. Drink garnish

4. _____ _____   4. Relish tray leftover

5. _____ _____   5. Refueling break

6. _____ _____   6. Slam on the brakes

7. _____ straw   7. What the loser drew

Answers on page 187.

Letter Sudoku

Solve this puzzle just as you would a sudoku. Use deductive logic to complete the grid so that each row, column, and 3 by 3 box contains the letters from the word COURTSHIP.

	P			I				
H				R		S		C
T					H		O	
		S			I		C	
C	O						I	P
	I		H			U		
	T		U					S
O		P		S				H
	S				C		T	

Letter Joust

Use the clues to solve the puzzle. When complete, the circled letters will spell out a mystery word.

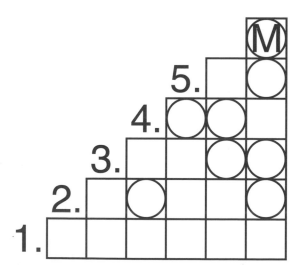

ACROSS

1. Winged monster
2. Dancing festival
3. Quick attack
4. Cauldron
5. To _____ or not to _____

Mystery word: _____

Answers on page 187.

Word Ladder

Use the clues to change just one letter on each line to go from the top word to the bottom word. Do not change the order of the letters. You must have a Scrabble word at each step.

1. TRAWL
_____ public fist fight
_____ read with your hands
_____ Galahad found it
_____ cereal
_____ wit
_____ strength
PRAWN

2. BLUNT
_____
_____
_____
_____
_____
_____
BRAND

Fitting Words with a P

In this miniature crossword, the clues are listed randomly and are numbered only for convenience. Figure out the placement of the 9 answers. To help you out, 1 letter is inserted in the grid, and this is the only occurrence of that letter in the completed puzzle.

CLUES
1. Restaurant posting
2. Hair salon items
3. Craze
4. Summer _____
5. Plunge a knife into
6. _____ bob
7. Fend off
8. Egg-shape
9. Top of cup

SCRABBLE

Overlapping Words

This puzzle works exactly like a crossword, only without the divisions between words. In fact, some words blend into one another, so solving one clue will help you solve another. Numbers indicate the boxes answers occupy.

1	2	3	4	5	6	7	8	9
32	33	34	35	36	37	38	39	10
31	56	57	58	59	60	61	40	11
30	55	72	73	74	75	62	41	12
29	54	71	80		76	63	42	13
28	53	70	79	78	77	64	43	14
27	52	69	68	67	66	65	44	15
26	51	50	49	48	47	46	45	16
25	24	23	22	21	20	19	18	17

1-4. Identical sibling

1-7. Muscle spasms

3-8. Take in, as food

7-11. Tricky maneuver

9-13. Up to this point

11-16. Leaning to one side

14-18. Woman's sleeveless undergarment

17-23. Family line of rulers

19-23. Unpleasant

22-27. Keyboard user

24-29. Detroit pro

27-33. Languages

30-39. Separate residence on an estate

34-37. You, formerly

38-43. Minute part

40-48. Orchestra leader

43-46. Enclosed conduit

46-51. Hot and sultry

49-53. Theme park attractions

51-57. Movement downward

54-59. Midpoint

58-62. Intensify suddenly

60-65. Positive trend

62-69. Pastry choice

66-73. Warm too much

70-76. Pagan

74-80. Nag

77-80. Quick kiss

T I P

Spellings of individual Greek and Hebrew letters are valid plays. So are Old English letters eth, wynn, and yogh.

Answers on page 187.

Rhyme It

Each clue leads to a 2-word answer that rhymes, such as BIG PIG or STABLE TABLE. The numbers in parentheses after the clue give the number of letters in each word. For example, "Cookware taken from the oven (3, 3)" would be HOT POT.

1. Angry alum (3, 4): _____ _____

2. No work for 24 hours (4, 3): _____ _____

3. Identification problem (4, 4): _____ _____

4. Dentist's order (4, 5): _____ _____

5. Judge's irritation (4, 5): _____ _____

6. Extremely unshaven (4, 5): _____ _____

7. Equal thirds, perhaps (4, 5): _____ _____

8. Beau's noncommittal response (5, 4): _____ _____

9. Vocalist's faux pas (5, 4): _____ _____

10. Biggest heartache (5, 5): _____ _____

11. Tennis or basketball (5, 5): _____ _____

12. Furniture item in storage (5, 5): _____ _____

13. Seem close (6, 4): _____ _____

14. Selling fake brand-name coats (6, 6): _____ _____

15. The case of the missing taper (6, 7): _____ _____

A Demanding Puzzle

Spell a 10-letter word by moving between adjacent letters. Every letter will be used at least once, but no letter will be used consecutively. Begin at any letter.

Answers on page 187.

What's the Catch?

Each rack of seven letters below forms exactly one valid seven-letter bingo word. Unscramble them to find the bingo, then find words with six, five, four, three, and two letters each to complete the puzzle.

Grid Fill

To complete this puzzle, place the given letters and words into the shapes on this grid. Words and letters will run across, down, and wrap around each shape. When the grid is filled, each row will contain one of the following words: alters, credit, hardly, needle, school, snappy, streak.

1. C₃ D₂ H₄ L₁

2. E₁ D₂ I₁ T₁ L₁ N₁
   P₃ D₂ P₃ Y₄ R₁ S₁

3. A₁ C₃ T₁ A₁ L₁ E₁
   A₁ S₁ H₄ E₁ R₁ E₁
   O₁ R₁ E₁

4. T₁ E₁ A₁ R₁
   Y₄ O₁ L₁ K₅

The best plays don't necessarily use all 7 tiles. Play "JEEZ" in the right spot for 84 points, or "QUIZ" for 96.

Answers on page 188.

Animal Riddles

Cryptograms are messages in substitution code. Break the code to read the riddles and their answers. THE SMART CAT might become FVO QWGDF JGF if F is substituted for T, V for H, O for E, and so on. The code is the same for both cryptograms.

1. IOGN UV MEGTR GJB IOUNW GJB "PWB" GEE QFWP?

   G LWMPG IWGPUJY EUHVNUTR.

2. IOK BUB NOW HQEUTW GPPWVN NOW MUPB?

   MWTGSVW UN IGV G PQMUJ.

From Soft to Hard

Use the clues to change just one letter on each line to go from the top word to the bottom word. Do not change the order of the letters. You must have a Scrabble word at each step.

SOFT

_____ type of

_____ painful

_____ apple center

_____ phone wire

_____ postal message

HARD

Answers on page 188.

Bowling Terms

Ignoring spaces, capitalization, and punctuation, find a bowling term in each of the sentences below.

1. "Strike up the band! It's time to march!" announced the bandleader, stepping out smartly as the band fell in behind him.

2. "I've been framed!" he accused the court, swearing his innocence as he was dragged from the room.

3. Stringent rules were put in place to stop any untoward behavior, but they did little to discourage Richard and Marjorie from breaking them all with gleeful abandon.

4. Arial was very pleased with her pinafore – it was such a lovely color.

5. "I want all eyes on the bride," the dressmaker explained.

6. Louis pared the apple efficiently as he discussed what else needed doing in order to be ready for the evening's extravaganza.

7. "Bob, all of them are gone!" shrieked Alice. "All that's left are a few empty eggshells."

8. "Be wary of cutting yourself with the knife," the television show chef advises as he deftly carves core and apple.

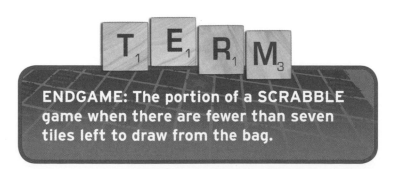

ENDGAME: The portion of a SCRABBLE game when there are fewer than seven tiles left to draw from the bag.

Answers on page 188.

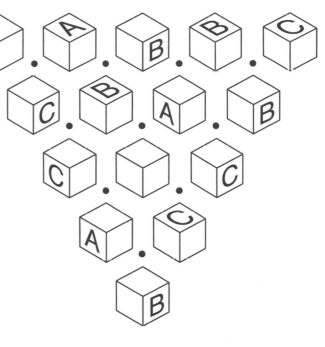

Letter Block Lock

Fill in each individual block with the letters A, B, and C. No letter should be adjacent to itself – horizontally or vertically – between blocks.

Get Fit

Fit the pieces into the frame to form Scrabble words reading across and down. There's no need to rotate the pieces; they'll fit as shown, with each piece used once.

      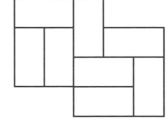

LI VE
CR SS
MU A T P
U   T A Y

The S is a powerful tile. Save it until you can use it to its full potential.

Answers on page 188.

Rhyme Time

Each clue leads to a 2-word answer that rhymes, such as BIG PIG or STABLE TABLE. The numbers in parentheses after the clue give the number of letters in each word. We've done the first one for you.

1. Underachiever's credo (3, 3): WHY TRY

2. They make meals for the masses (4, 4): _____ _____

3. She can afford the best of brooms (4, 5): _____ _____

4. Attorney's excessive billing (4, 5): _____ _____

5. Aid for river crossers (4, 5): _____ _____

6. It's got a whistle too (5, 4): _____ _____

7. Time stopper (5, 4): _____ _____

8. They're hooked on omelets (6, 5): _____ _____

9. Revolutionary new pedal (6, 5): _____ _____

10. Require the study of poetry (6, 5): _____ _____

11. How to avoid dog bites (6, 6): _____ _____

12. Where to find roots (7, 5): _____ _____

13. Underachiever's credo (5, 8): _____ _____

14. In search of comic relief (5, 8): _____ _____

15. Monotonous tiles (6, 8): _____ _____

Holiday Wordplay

There are 14 letters in "Merry Christmas." But if you count each different letter just once, there are only 10 unique letters. Can you rearrange those 10 letters to form a high school subject and the top grade a good student would get in it?

Answers on page 188.

Alphabet Fill-In

The first and last letters have been left off of the 13 five-letter words below. Your task is to complete each word, using each letter of the alphabet only once. The first has been done to get you started.

1. SOLID
2. ___HAK___
3. ___AYO___
4. ___ENO___
5. ___ELA___
6. ___UNT___
7. ___ILC___

8. ___UER___
9. ___GRE___
10. ___REE___
11. ___LUM___
12. ___HAR___
13. ___ING___

Letter Powwow

Spell a 10-letter word by moving between adjacent letters. Every letter will be used at least once, but no letter will be used consecutively. Begin at any letter.

Answers on page 188.

Blocked In

Fit the words into the grid reading across and down. Each word is used once.

DEER   PRIDE
EIDER   RITE
ERRS   STEER
IDEA   TEARS
PEST

Game On!

Solve this puzzle just as you would a sudoku puzzle. Use deductive logic to complete the grid so that each row, column, and 2 by 2 box contains the letters from the word G A M E.

			A
		M	
A			
			G

Sanctioned tournament games are timed. Each player has 25 minutes to play the entire game. Players are penalized 10 points per minute over the allotted 25.

Answers on page 188.

Before You Sip

Four 7-letter words, all of which revolve around the same theme, have been jumbled. Unscramble each word, and write the answer in the accompanying space. Next, transfer the letters in the shaded boxes into the shaded keyword space, and unscramble the 5-letter word that goes with the theme. The theme for this puzzle is wine.

Answers on page 188.

SCRABBLE
Crossword Game

The Cogs of War

Each rack of seven letters below forms exactly one valid seven-letter bingo word. Unscramble them to find the bingo, then find words with six, five, four, three, and two letters each to complete the puzzle.

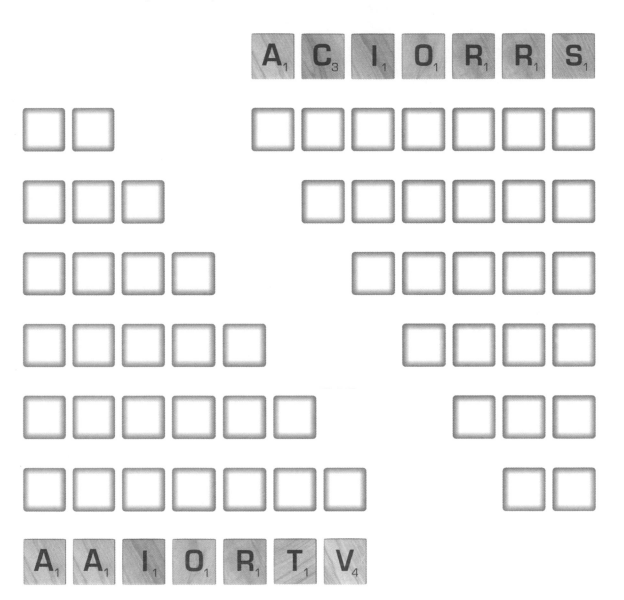

Word Ladders

Change just one letter on each line to go from the top word to the bottom word.
Do not change the order of the letters. You must have a Scrabble word at each step.

1. FOOT

———
———
———
———

BALL

3. SIDE

———
———
———

WALK

2. SNOW

———
———
———
———

FORT

4. LEFT

———
———
———

HAND

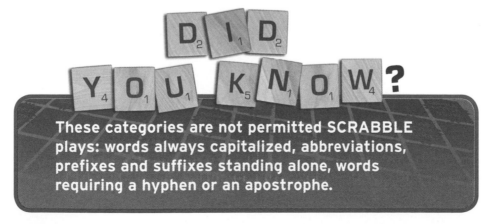

DID YOU KNOW?

These categories are not permitted SCRABBLE plays: words always capitalized, abbreviations, prefixes and suffixes standing alone, words requiring a hyphen or an apostrophe.

Answers on page 189.

Make the Cut

Use the clues to solve the puzzle. When complete, the circled letters will spell out a mystery word.

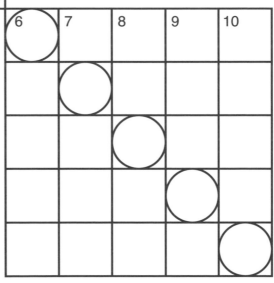

ACROSS
1. Small liquid units
2. Seat of emotion
3. Teacher's present
4. Quick
5. Not urban

DOWN
6. On high
7. Bend over
8. Shop
9. Flaming
10. Tale

Mystery word clue:
Hair remover

Answers on page 189.

Word Pyramid

Fill in the word pyramid by finding the answer to each clue and writing it on the corresponding step. As you move from the top down, each new word is an anagram of the previous word, with one letter added.

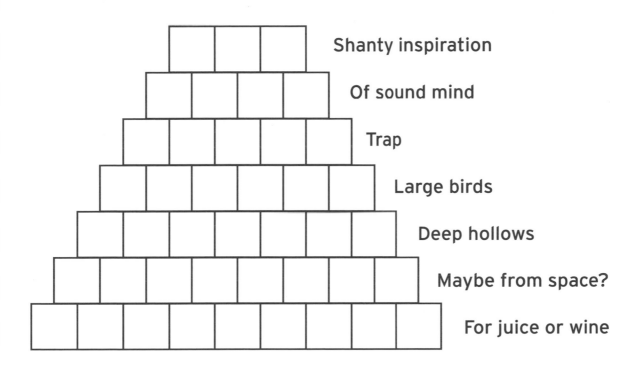

Shanty inspiration

Of sound mind

Trap

Large birds

Deep hollows

Maybe from space?

For juice or wine

A Twisted Wrister

Fit the pieces into the frame to form Scrabble words reading across and down. There's no need to rotate the pieces; they'll fit as shown, with each piece used once.

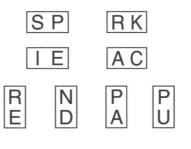

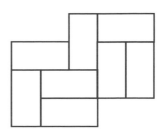

Answers on page 189.

W₄ O₁ R₁ D₂

Wordstrain

Write the answer to each clue in the grid below, beginning each word in the square with its corresponding number. Words will overlap.

1. Ball thrower

2. Chubby angel

3. Bombing aftermath

4. Whiten

5. Causing discomfort

6. Swallow

7. Alienate the affections of

8. "The Lone _____"

9. European language

10. Isle of _____

| 1 | | 2 | | 3 | | 4 | | 5 | | 6 | | 7 | | 8 | | 9 | | 10 | | |

Word Weft

Fit the words into the grid reading across and down. Each word is used once. One letter have been given to get you started.

E

ERRS   RIDE
IDLE   RIDER
IDLER   TRIP
PEEL   TRIPE
PEELS

T₁ I₁ P₃

Always look for places to get 4x or 6x the value of a J, Q, X or Z.

Answers on page 189.

Musical Chairs

Each rack of seven letters below forms exactly one valid seven-letter bingo word. Unscramble them to find the bingo, then find words with six, five, four, three, and two letters each to complete the puzzle.

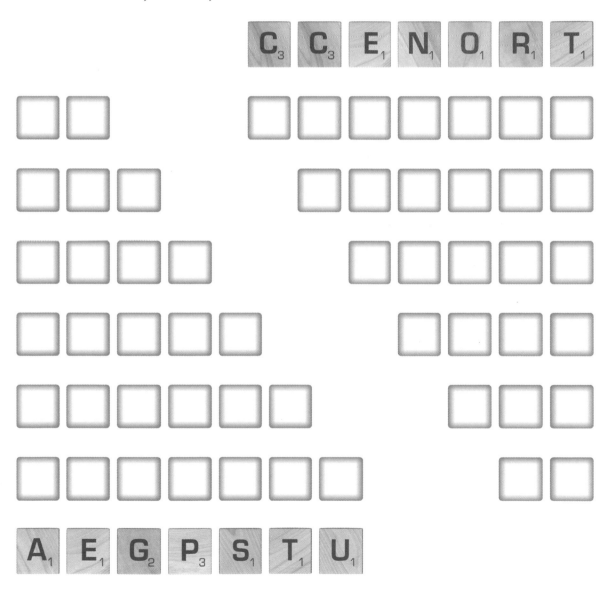

C₃ C₃ E₁ N₁ O₁ R₁ T₁

A₁ E₁ G₂ P₃ S₁ T₁ U₁

Answers on page 189.

Similar Lines

Each of these groups contains a simile ("___ as a ___") within it. Decipher the similes by moving from letter to letter. Some letters will be used more than once, and you may have to double back on some lines. For example: sly as a fox

1.

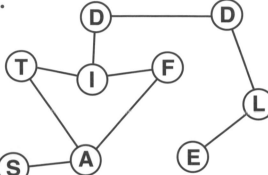

2.

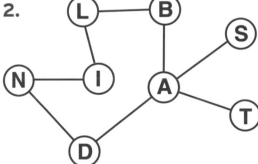

3.

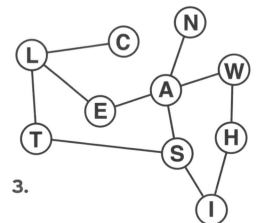

4.

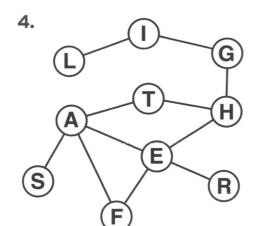

5.

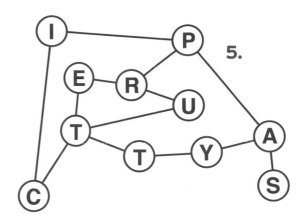

6.

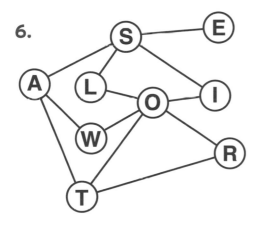

7.

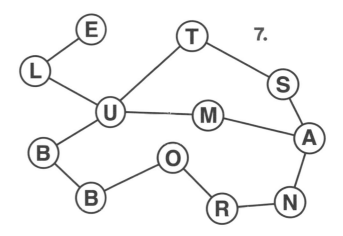

Answers on page 189.

Odd One Out

Can you determine which of the words below is the odd one out?
Hint: Think about pronunciations and meanings.

Cast-a-Word

There are 4 dice, and there are different letters of the alphabet on the 6 faces of each of them (each letter appears only once). Random throws of the dice produced the words in this list. Can you figure out which letters appear on each of the 4 dice?

BADE	LOAF
CROW	MILK
ESPY	PAST
FOLK	PERK
FOXY	QUAD
HOLD	VINE
HUGE	WINK
KILO	

BLUFFING: The act of deliberately playing a phoney word. This is completely ethical and is a weapon used by many experts, even against other experts.

Answers on page 189.

Addagram

This puzzle functions exactly like an anagram with an added step: In addition to being scrambled, each word below is missing the same letter. Discover the missing letter, then unscramble the words.

1. When you do, you'll reveal a male astronaut, a muscle, a type of ship, and a room.

CANAPES   EATERS

TRASHING   BRACEH

2. When you do, you'll reveal a wild pig found in Africa, a mythical sea creature, a seed often added to bread, and a treatment performed on the hands.

GROWTH   SEEMS

DIMMER   NUMERIC

HOOK: A letter that will spell a new word when it is played in front of or at the end of a word on the board. With HARD on the board, the letter Y is a hook letter since HARDY is acceptable. Likewise the letter C, since CHARD is acceptable.

Answers on page 189.

Elevator Words

Like an elevator, words move up and down the "floors" of this puzzle. Starting with the first answer, the second part of each answer carries down to become the first part of the following answer. With the clues given, complete the puzzle.

1. Quick _____
2. _____ _____
3. _____ _____
4. _____ _____
5. _____ _____
6. _____ _____
7. _____ defense

1. She adjusts rapidly
2. Learner's aid
3. It's found at the top of the page in a reference book
4. Document production
5. How long it takes to complete a procedure
6. One of 24 that circle the globe
7. Hoops strategy

A Measure of Deception

Find the hidden phrase by using the letters directly below each of the blank squares. Each letter is used only once. A black square or the end of the line indicates the end of a word.

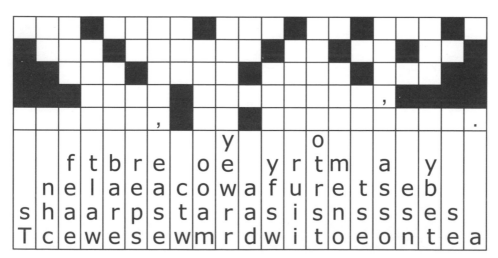

Answers on page 190.

Say What?

Below is a group of words that, when properly arranged in the blanks, reveal a quote from a famous figure.

IDEA   HAS   REVOLUTION   BAYONETS   ITS   IS

A _____ _____ an _____ which _____ found _____ _____

A Nice Trait to Have

Spell a 10-letter word by moving between adjacent letters. Every letter will be used at least once, but no letter will be used consecutively. Begin at any letter.

TURNOVER: Players are going for "turnover" when they play as many tiles as possible in order to draw as many new tiles as possible. If you played 60 tiles in a game, you had a 60% chance of drawing the good tiles.

STEMS: Certain five- and six-letter combinations of letters are so useful for forming bingos that lists of bingos have been printed that use these five- and six-letter stems.

Answers on page 190.

Scrambled Identity

These seven letters spell exactly one valid seven-letter Scrabble word. Can you find it?

C₃ E₁ M₃ O₁ S₁ T₁ U₁

6-Letter Circles

Answer each clue with a 6-letter word. Write the words in a clockwise direction around the numerals in the grid. Words overlap each other and may start in any of the spaces around the numerals. We've placed some letters to get you started.

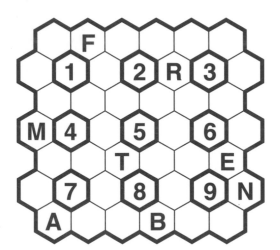

1. Inform
2. Hardly ever
3. Place inside
4. Like a citrus fruit
5. Frivolity
6. Creates cloth
7. Take a trip
8. Tasty morsel
9. Virgil's epic poem

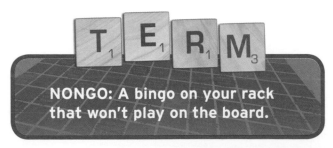

T₁ E₁ R₁ M₃

NONGO: A bingo on your rack that won't play on the board.

Answers on page 190.

Carpe Diem

Each rack of seven letters below forms exactly one valid seven-letter bingo word. Unscramble them to find the bingo, then find words with six, five, four, three, and two letters each to complete the puzzle.

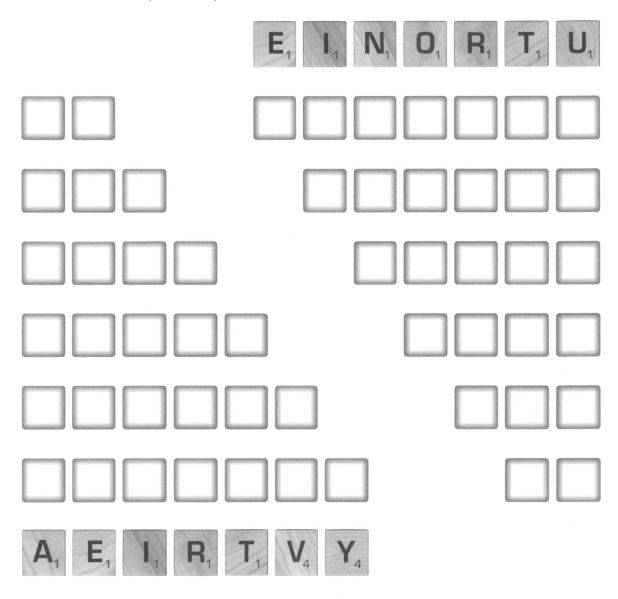

Cast-a-Word

There are 4 dice, and there are different letters of the alphabet on the 6 faces of each of them (each letter appears only once). Random throws of the dice produced the words in this list. Can you figure out which letters appear on each of the 4 dice?

BLIP	PLUG
CAPE	SCAM
DOWN	SLIM
FARM	STAY
GASH	VOID
GRAM	WRIT
JAGS	ZIPS
KNOB	

Chomp Romp

Each clue leads to a 2-word answer that rhymes, such as BIG PIG or STABLE TABLE. The numbers in parentheses after the clue give the number of letters in each word. For example, "cookware taken from the oven (3, 3)" would be HOT POT.

1. A little jog before all that eating (3,3): _____ _____

2. The butter when it's first put on the corn (3,4): _____ _____

3. They entertained superbly before the fireworks (5,4): _____ _____

4. Arrive at the sandy place where the picnic is being held (5,5): _____ _____

5. The place from which many seaside fireworks are set off (5,5): _____ _____

6. Avoids a salty picnic side dish (5,5): _____ _____

7. Holiday address about a popular summer fruit (5,6): _____ _____

8. Souvenir collection starting with the original 13 (6,6): _____ _____

9. Purchase from a music show (7,5): _____ _____

Answers on page 190.

Sweetheart Scramble

Four 7-letter words, all of which revolve around the same theme, have been jumbled. Unscramble each word, and write the answer in the accompanying space. Next, transfer the letters in the shaded boxes into the shaded keyword space, and unscramble the 9-letter word that goes with the theme. The theme for this puzzle is romance.

Grid Fill

To complete this puzzle, place the given letters and words into the shapes in this grid. Words and letters will run across, down, and wrap around each shape. When the grid is filled, each row will contain one of the following words: Attire, Blinds, Finite, Garage, Hourly, Lapsed, Overly.

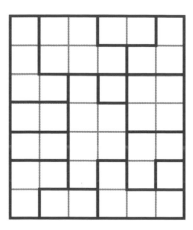

1. D, I

2. AR, FI, HO, ND

3. LAG, SLY, TEE

4. BOAT, RELY, SAGE

5. LIVER

6. TURNIP

Shell Game

These seven letters spell exactly one valid seven-letter Scrabble word. Can you find it?

If an unacceptable word is not challenged when it's played, it will stay on the board for the remainder of the game.

Answers on page 190.

Permission Granite

Each rack of seven letters below forms exactly one valid seven-letter bingo word. Unscramble them to find the bingo, then find words with six, five, four, three, and two letters each to complete the puzzle.

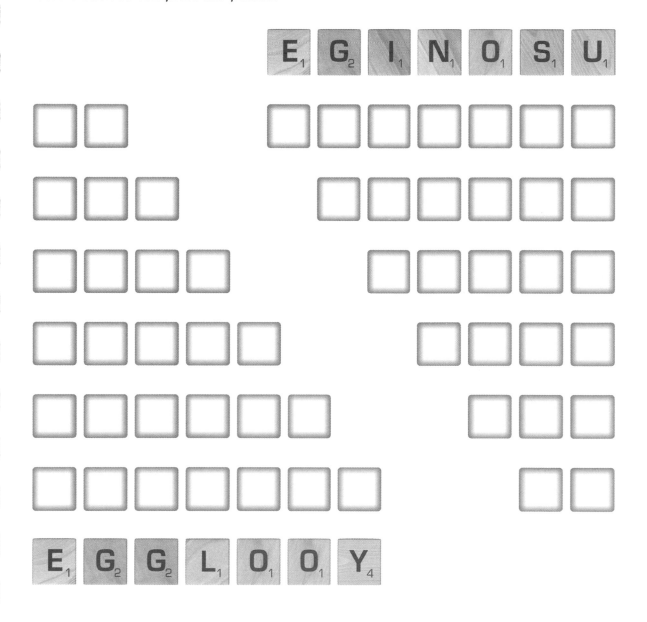

Fast Food

Fill in the blank spaces as you would a crossword puzzle. The theme — or title — of the puzzle might appear to be ambiguous, but it should suggest a category of words that, when linked together, will complete the puzzle.

For example, HOLE IN ONE might suggest DOUGHNUTS. Or, it might suggest GOLF, which would lead to the words CLUB, IRON, TEE, etc. But all of these words have a common theme. Notice that a few letters are already in place, and some of the words intersect — adding to the mystery, and the fun, of finding the solution.

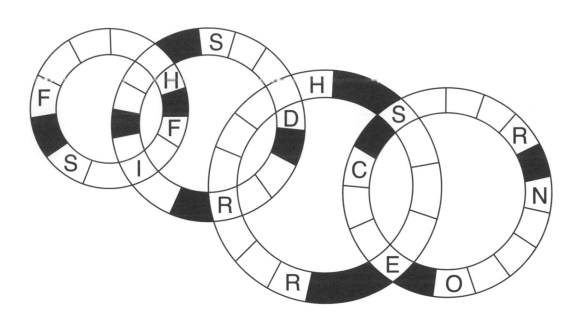

Word Jigsaw

Fit the pieces into the frame to form Scrabble words reading across and down. There's no need to rotate the pieces; they'll fit as shown, with each piece used once.

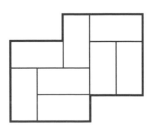

Answers on pages 190-191.

Puzzle Pilgrim

Solve this puzzle just as you would a sudoku. Use deductive logic to complete the grid so that each row, column, and 3 by 3 box contains the letters the term MAYFLOWER.

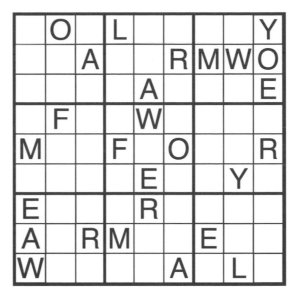

Stand and Deliver

Use the clues to solve the puzzle. When complete, the circled letters will spell out a mystery word.

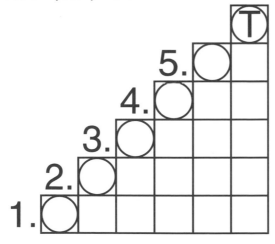

ACROSS

1. Church official
2. Beneath
3. Authority figure
4. Fiery place
5. Not out

Mystery word: _____

Answers on page 191.

Comrade Calamity

Find the hidden quote from Mark Twain by using the letters directly below each of the blank squares. Each letter is used only once. A black square indicates the end of a word.

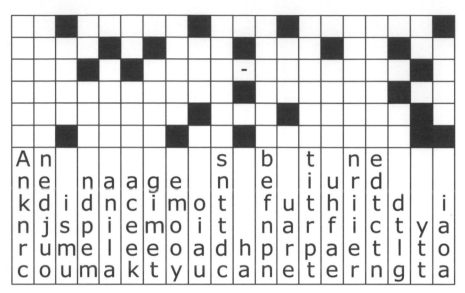

Abundant S's

Fit the given words into the crossword grid.

EDIT
HA
SALAD
SASS
SHE
SIN
SLAIN
STINT
TI (musical note)

Answers on page 191.

Coif-Doku

Solve this puzzle just as you would a
sudoku puzzle. Use deductive logic to
complete the grid so that each row,
column, and 3 by 3 box contains the letters
from the words HAIR STYLE.

	A	H			T	R		
	L		R	I			A	
	T	H						
T	A		I					
		S		Y				
			T		Y			L
			H	L				
E		T	S		I			
	R	L			S	Y		

Puzzle Buzzle

Each clue leads to a 2-word answer that rhymes, such as BIG PIG or STABLE TABLE.
The numbers in parentheses after the clue give the number of letters in each word.
For example, "cookware taken from the oven (3, 3)" would be HOT POT.

1. Soar at great elevation (3, 4): _____ _____

2. Extra seat (5, 5): _____ _____

3. Regulation around the swimming area (4, 4): _____ _____

4. Receives dogs, cats and fish (4, 4): _____ _____

5. Orderly lines of beautiful red flowers (4, 4): _____ _____

6. Circus performer's sad expression (5, 5): _____ _____

7. Young bird with an illness (4, 5): _____ _____

8. Flimsier-than-average barrier around tomatoes, grapes, or people (4, 4): _____ _____

9. What shovels do in February (5, 4): _____ _____

10. Ran by after everyone else (6, 4): _____ _____

11. Small wind instrument, when silent (4, 5): _____ _____

12. What Superman might use to repair his costume (4, 4): _____ _____

Answers on page 191.

Math Scramblegram

Four 6-letter words, all of which revolve around the same theme, have been jumbled. Unscramble each word, and write the answer in the accompanying space. Next, transfer the letters in the shaded boxes into the shaded keyword space, and unscramble the 8-letter word that goes with the theme. The theme for this puzzle is mathematics.

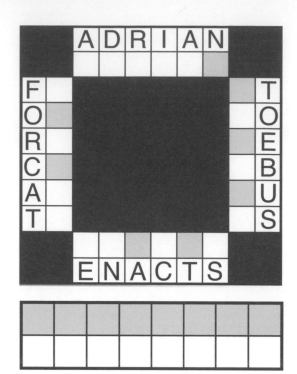

This Game Is Wild!

Use the clues to solve the puzzle. When complete, the circled letters will spell out a mystery word.

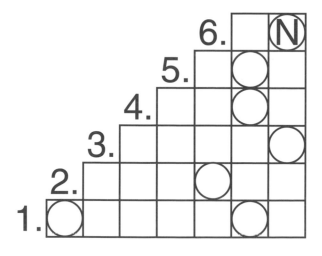

ACROSS

1. Wild animal
2. Forest paths
3. Hunting weapon
4. Where game hides
5. Hunter's best friend
6. Hunt is over, coming _____

Mystery word: _____

Answers on page 191.

Hidden Word

Hidden below is a Scrabble word. Unscramble the letters to discover what it is.

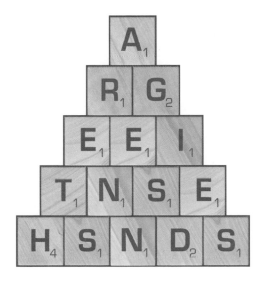

This Will Irritate

Spell a 10-letter word by moving between adjacent letters. Every letter will be used at least once, but no letter will be used consecutively. Begin at any letter.

Two-letter words using high-point letters: AX, EX, JO, QI, XI, XU, and ZA.

Answers on page 192.

SCRABBLE
Crossword Game

W O R D

Add One Letter

This is a standard word search with a twist: For each word in the list, you must add one letter to form a new word, which you will then search for in the grid. For example: If the listed word is CARTON, you'd search for CARTOON; if the listed word is OTTER, you might have to search for HOTTER or POTTER. The words can be found in a straight line horizontally, vertically, or diagonally, and may read forward or backward.

AMPLE   GROW

ARBOR   HUNCHES

ASTERN   LACING

AUGHT   PLACE

BATH   SAVING

BEACH   SCENT

CACHES   SENATE

CANDID   SORT

CAVE   STATE

CEMENT   TAILED

EASE   TEMPS

ELATE   VALE

FILL

```
H L R B T E M P T S B R X
H C A E R B S H A V I N G
E A S T E R N C B L H X Z
T N E M E L C T A A A J L
A D H Q O A N A R E T C S
S I C E M E S B D L R Y E
N E N P C F O E V A R C H
E D U S R R L S D X M A C
S L A C K I N G T I Y P A
E N H V A L V E S A R E O
L W O R G L X D Y B T F C
M X T R E L A T E K D U O
J F L P T A U G H T I S E
```

Answers on page 192.

Step to It

Enter every letter of the alphabet into the grid. Letters are connected horizontally, vertically, or diagonally from A to Z. Use the clue to fill in the circles and help complete the grid.

Clue: Footwear tie

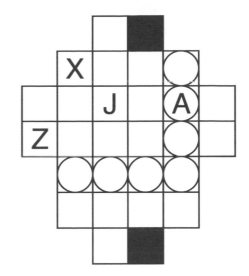

Today's Special

Fill in each empty box with a different letter so a trio of related words is formed.

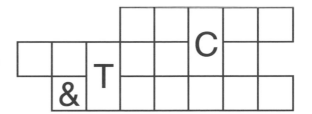

T E R M

BLOCKING: Playing a word that stops the opponent from making a potentially large score, or playing words that make it harder for either player to score many points.

Answers on page 192.

Like New

Use the clues to solve the puzzle. When complete, the circled letters will spell out a mystery word.

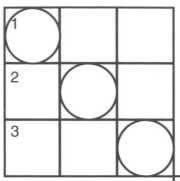

ACROSS
1. Large, jellylike drop
2. Ancient
3. Scarer's declaration

DOWN
4. A small taste
5. Venomous snake
6. Fifth month

Mystery word clue:
Very shiny

Elevator Words

Like an elevator, words move up and down the "floors" of this puzzle. Starting with the first answer, the second part of each answer carries down to become the first part of the following answer. With the clues given, complete the puzzle.

1. Jumbo _____
2. _____ _____
3. _____ _____
4. _____ _____
5. _____ _____
6. _____ _____
7. _____ language

1. 747, for one
2. Personal water craft
3. Ride up the snow-covered slope
4. Roadside rescue vehicle
5. A place for refueling on the highway
6. Street-light alternative
7. Communication using hand gestures

Answers on page 192.

Tidbit Words

Fit the given words into the crossword grid.

AD	MISSION
AT	MOB
ATE	NET
BOA	SOP
DRAM	STRIKES
EAT	TAM
ITEMS	TIC
LA	TO
MET	TOIL

Bingo!

Rearrange ZINCITE to spell one other valid seven-letter Scrabble word.

DID YOU KNOW?

Today the SCRABBLE game is found in three of every five American homes.

The total face value of all the SCRABBLE tiles is 187.

Answers on page 192.

Textiles

Four 6-letter words, all of which revolve around the same theme, have been jumbled. Unscramble each word, and write the answer in the accompanying space. Next, transfer the letters in the shaded boxes into the shaded keyword spaces, and unscramble the 8-letter word that goes with the theme. The theme for this puzzle is fabrics.

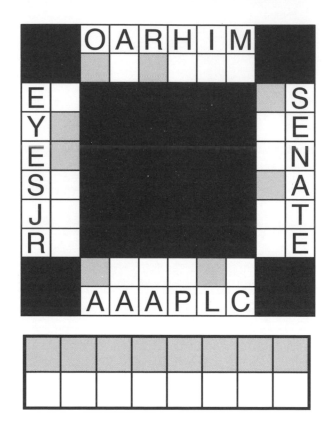

Word Assembly

Fit the pieces into the frame to form Scrabble words reading across and down. There's no need to rotate the pieces; they'll fit as shown, with each piece used once.

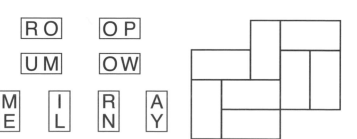

Answers on page 192.

Harmonic Convergence

Each rack of seven letters below forms exactly one valid seven-letter bingo word. Unscramble them to find the bingo, then find words with six, five, four, three, and two letters each to complete the puzzle.

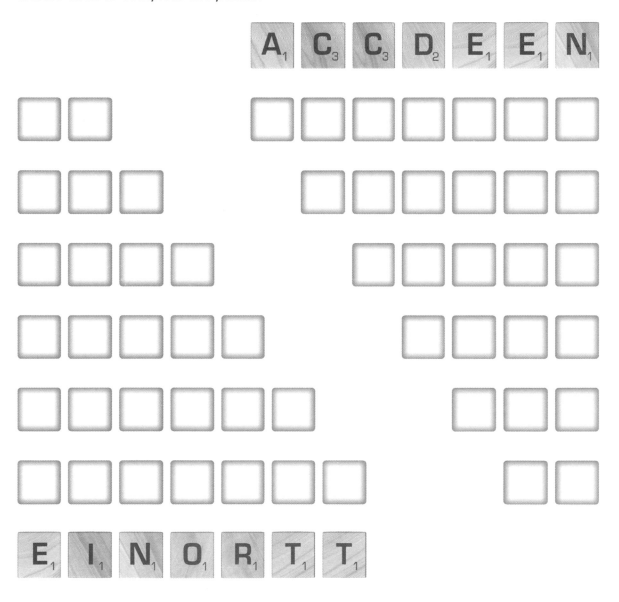

Answers

Crossword Twist (page 2)

```
S T O N E
  O     N
S O L I D
E     L
E V I L S
```

Finely Fit (page 2)

```
H O L E Y
U V U L A
R E A L M
T R U S S
```

Word for Bird (page 3)

T [EDITION] D

U [YOUNGER] I

R [RAVIOLI] N

K [TADPOLE] N

E [KINDRED] E

Y [UTOPIAN] R

Makes a Kind of Sense (page 4)
It's downright annoying to argue with a guy who knows what he is talking about.

Fabulous Cryptids (page 4)
1. UNICORN; 2. DRAGON;
3. MINOTAUR; 4. CENTAUR;
5. MERMAID; 6. GRIFFIN

Put Your Finger on It (page 5)

```
M A N O R
S A I N T
I N N E R
T U L I P
M U S I C
```

```
U P S F T
N R A I R
D A I R E
E N L S A
R K S T T
```

Shall I Compare Thee... (page 6)
EIMNOSW: 1. WINSOME; 2. EONISM;
3. MINES; 4. IONS; 5. EON; 6. EM

AEHLPSY: 1. SHAPELY; 2. ALEPHS;
3. HEAPY; 4. PEAL; 5. ALP; 6. SH

Word Jigsaw (page 7)

1.
```
  H U M
E R A S E
V A L E T
E G O
```

2.
```
    Z O O
S T E I N
A I S L E
W E T
```

Spoken Well (page 8)

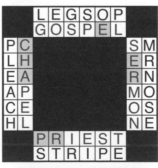

```
  L E G S O P
  G O S P E L
P C           S M
L H           E R
E A           R N
A P           M O
C E           O S
H L           N E
  P R I E S T
  S T R I P E
```

```
E C H A E R P R
P R E A C H E R
```

Answers

Better to Give (page 9)

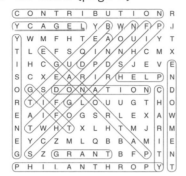

Wedge the Words (page 10)

Rather Numerous (page 10)

POPULOUSLY

Ways to Move (page 10)

Across and Down (page 11)

MACHO
AGLOW
NOOSE
EGGED

Alphabet Menagerie (page 11)

There's an Art to It (page 12)

Paint By Numbers (page 13)

ACDELNO; 1. CELADON; 2. LOANED;
3. ALONE; 4. CODE; 5. NAE; 6. EL

ACFHISU: 1. FUCHSIA; 2. FICHUS;
3. FICUS; 4. SUCH; 5. CHI; 6. IF

Code-doku (page 14)

T	O	H	U	M
H	U	M	T	O
M	T	O	H	U
O	H	U	M	T
U	M	T	O	H

Forward Thinking (page 14)

FRONTAL

Flying High (page 15)

COANFL	FALCON
RIOBN	ROBIN
CAALINRD	CARDINAL
NAARYC	CANARY
BIRDULEB	BLUEBIRD
WOCR	CROW
EGLAE	EAGLE
WSROPRA	SPARROW
GASLIRNT	STARLING

FREE AS A BIRD

Answers

Split Decisions (page 16)

Answers may vary.

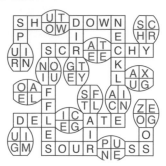

Scrambled Letters (page 16)

GEOGRAPHICALLY

A to Z (page 17)

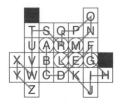

It's in the Drawer (page 17)

The missing letter is R.
Grater, strainer, can opener,
garlic press

Get Moving! (page 17)

A Spot of Starch (page 18)

Scratch It Out (page 18)

CHICKEN

Circular Words (page 19)

MANIFEST, APPARENT

Add-a-Letter (pages 20–21)

From A to Z (page 22)

Addagram (page 23)

1. The missing letter is Y.
Typhoon, hysteria, asylum, mainstay
2. The missing letter is N.
Artisan, container, nectar, entangle

One Word Leads to Another
(page 23)

Answers

Find the Perfect Fit (page 24)

Combing for Clues (page 24)

Put It All Together
(page 25)

Mystery word: **SHOPPERS**

7. I F O
6. H A T
5. C A F E
4. P R I M P
3. J E W E L S
2. E M E R A L D
1. E N S E M B L E

Classical Talent (page 25)
SYMPHONY/ORCHESTRA

A Cut Above (page 26)
**BEIKRST: 1. BRISKET; 2. BIKERS;
3. SKIER; 4. SKIT; 5. BIT; 6. BI**

**EINNOSV: 1. VENISON; 2. OVINES;
3. NOISE; 4. VINE; 5. VIE; 6. ON**

Wise Words (page 27)

Most of us are loyal – when we reach a certain age we like to stick to it.

The things most people want to know are none of their business.

Nothing is impossible to the man who does not have to do it himself.

Thinking well is wise; planning well is wiser; doing well is wisest and best of all.

You can keep your head above water if you hold your chin up.

Success is knowing the difference between cornering people and getting them in your corner.

Birthday Food (page 28)

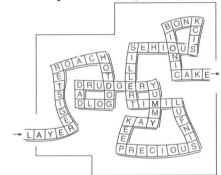

Lots of Air (page 29)

Moral Fiber (page 30)
**ACGINOR: 1. ORGANIC; 2. CARING;
3. CARGO; 4. GAIN; 5. RAG; 6. OR**

**AALNRTU: 1. NATURAL; 2. ANURAL;
3. NATAL; 4. AURA; 5. URN; 6. AR**

Answers

Word Ladder (page 31)

Answers may vary.

1. DRUNK, trunk, thunk, thank, shank, spank, stank, STAND

2. BRINE, bride, pride, prize, PRIME

Anagrams (page 31)

1. dad/add; 2. May/yam; 3. raw/war;
4. end/den; 5. ate/tea

Crazy Mixed-Up Letters (page 32)

3: hornets, shorten, thrones

The Perfect Way to Say It (page 32)

"Do not go where the path may lead, go instead where there is no path and leave a trail."

Answer the Homophone (page 32)

RIGHTS, RITES

Classical Music Makers (page 33)

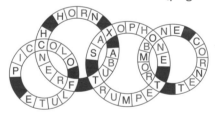

Add-a-Letter (pages 34–35)

Let's Puzzle! (page 36)

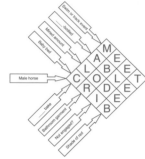

Pinwheel (page 37)

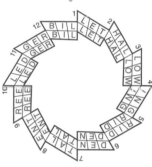

Seamless Spiral (pages 38-39)

```
R E S T R I N G I
O N N E T W O R N
S E R B I L K K G
S G O W B A I O E
E I R N   R N U R
L T C I A G G T U
G S S E M O D L N
N E V L A H T E D
I T S U O R E N O
```

It's Superlative (page 39)

AWESOME

Word Ladder (page 40)

Answers may vary.

1. PINK, rink, risk, rise, ROSE
2. JADE, wade, wide, wine, wing, RING
3. COOK, coop, chop, chow, chew, CHEF
4. FOOD, fond, fend, mend, MENU

Borrowed Words (page 41)

1. octopus, 2. porcupine, 3. pizza,

4. iceberg, 5. cabbage, 6. spaghetti,

7. ball, 8. ketchup, 9. fence, 10. cookie,

11. mosquito, 12. umbrella

Answers

Addagram (page 42)

1. The mystery letter is M.
Flamingo, platinum, comedy, remnant

2. The missing letter is Y.
Hockey, parsley, underlay, syndicate

Link and Lock (page 42)

Hone Your Rhymes (page 43)

1. flag bag; 2. slaw flaw; 3. fair share; 4. patio snow; 5. address mess; 6. backyard bard; 7. states debates; 8. parade brigade; 9. nation duration; 10. oration elation; 11. baseball for all; 12. color guard yard; 13. embellish relish; 14. declaration creation; 15. independence sentence

Find the Younger One (page 43)
DESCENDENT

Plus Code (page 44)

1. child; 2. extol; 3. event; 4. white; 5. byway; 6. ionic; 7. kudos; 8. zones; 9. usurp; 10. cycle

Anagrammed to Homonyms
(page 44)

Real/reel; leek/leak; lane/lain; meat/meet; soar/sore

The Fruit Vendor's Cart (page 45)

In a Stew (page 46)

carrot, turnip, pasta, potato, seasoning, leek, chicken, celery

Rhyme Time (page 47)

1. wind kind; 2. hard yard; 3. warm dorm; 4. tram scam; 5. pork fork; 6. rare chair; 7. regal eagle; 8. sweet treat; 9. troupe group; 10. groovy movie; 11. dental rental; 12. skeeter meter

Every Letter Plus Two Numbers (page 47)

Word Ladder (page 48)
Answers may vary.
1. There are two possible answers.
HATE, date, dote, dove, LOVE;
HATE, have, hive, live, LOVE.
2. DOVE, love, lore, lure, lurk, LARK

Where Are the Animals? (page 48)

1. dog, cat; 2. skunk, elk; 3. deer, owl; 4. fox, snake; 5. wolf, horse; 6. rabbit, elephant; 7. tiger, lion; 8. monkey, eagle; 9. seal, whale; 10. parrot, eel

Answers

Our Loopy Lingo (page 49)

I F		Y O U		H A	V E		A	B U N C H		O
F	O D D S		A N D		E N D S		A N D		G
E T		R I D		O F		A L L		B U T		O N E
O F		T H	E M ,		W H	A T		D O		Y O U
H A	V E ?									

What Did He Say? (page 49)

"Happiness can only be found if you can free yourself of all other distractions."

Know Your ABCs (page 50)

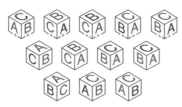

Fair Ball (page 50)

"This game is the only orderly thing in a very unorderly world. If you get three strikes, even the best lawyer in the world can't get you off."

All Squared (page 51)

S	A	L	T	S
A	W	A	I	T
L	A	R	G	E
T	I	G	E	R
S	T	E	R	N

A Nonstop State (page 51)

It's Political (page 51)

FASCISM

Play Ball! (page 52)

1. worth/throw; 2. aloft/float;
3. rated/trade; 4. idles/slide;
5. steal/least; 6. pleat/plate

Nip to It (page 52)

Mystery word: POWDER

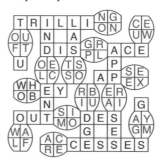

5. OH Ⓡ
4. NET
3. POST
2. CROWⒹ
1. SCRAⓅE

Exterior Design (page 53)

ACOPRRT: 1. CARPORT; 2. RAPTOR;
3. ACTOR; 4. TACO; 5. OPA; 6. TO

ADNORTU: 1. ROTUNDA; 2. AROUND;
3. DONUT; 4. ROAD; 5. ADO; 6. NU

Elevator Words (page 54)

1. INERT gas; 2. gas jet; 3. jet black; 4. blackjack; 5. jackknife; 6. knife blade; 7. blade ROAST

Petalgrams (page 54)

officer, magnify, alfalfa, uniform, refusal, leaflet
BONUS WORD: formula

Split Decisions (page 55)

Answers may vary.

Answers

Spin-o-Rama (page 56)

S	H	O	T	G
E	T	R	A	O
M	I	D	P	A
A	O	Z	E	L
G	E	N	O	Z

Bookend Letters (page 57)

SEATS; YEARLY; DELUDED; LEVEL; REVOLVER

Spin the Dials (page 57)

See image. The word is POCKET.

Inter-Textural (page 58)

ABDEILP: 1. PIEBALD; 2. ALIPED; 3. PALED; 4. BILE; 5. DIP; 6. PI

ACGINRZ: 1. CRAZING; 2. RAZING; 3. ACING; 4. ZINC; 5. ZIG; 6. ZA

Words with Purpose (page 59)

An Inward Spiral (pages 60–61)

A Quick One, to Start (page 62)

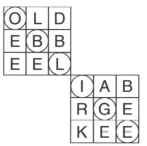

Anagrammatically Correct (page 63)

1. this/hits; 2. toms/most; 3. left/felt; 4. tale/late; 5. acre/race; 6. sore/rose; 7. cats/cast/acts; 8. snap/pans/naps

An Obvious Answer (page 63)

EVIDENT

Word Web (pages 64)

Answers

Word Jigsaw (page 65)

```
  G O O D
  P L A N E S
  P R O T E C T S
  R O B S   K I T E
  P A C E   F O R
  L I E S   F U R S
  U S E   T O O
  R E D   R U R A L
  A S     P O T A T O
  L       B E Y O N D
```

Word Ladder (page 66)

Answers may vary.

1. SNAP, slap, slat, slot, SHOT;
2. MILK, mill, mall, mail, PAIL;
3. LAKE, lane, land, lend, lead, MEAD;
4. SAIL, soil, coil, coal, coat, BOAT;
5. ROSE, ruse, rude, dude, duds, BUDS

Link Them (page 66)

O F F E N D U R E

Rhyme Time (page 67)

1. slow flow; 2. fish dish; 3. play away;
4. sole goal; 5. full bull; 6. pail tale;
7. worn horn; 8. wide slide; 9. ghost host;
10. third word; 11. horse force;
12. border order; 13. madder adder;
14. better letter; 15. colder shoulder

Tangled Words (pages 68–69)

```
A T E E W S R E T T I B S
S L L O T A G N I P M O R
S O P U Z A P P E D M E E
E J M H L R E F L E X E S
S P A O A R R R E E S G T
S D R A O B P U C R C N A
E E T L P R E U I O A U U
R E P R I N T T F V R L R
G X N V E E U P I R C P A
E O A V T L A L R A E S N
N T I C Y C L I C A L A T
E L I N E A R I A A Y L K
S L U D G E Y S S A B M E
```

Addagram (page 70)

1. The missing letter is R.
Arsenic, gardener, ramble, nurture
2. The missing letter is O.
Oregano, nougat, asteroid, outsider

Network (page 70)

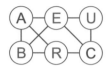

Avian Home (page 71)

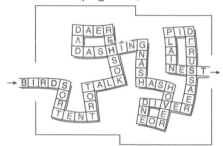

Pharmacy Fountain (page 72)

Pillers of Society (page 73)

CDEEINO: 1. CODEINE; 2. COINED;
3. CONED; 4. ICON; 5. CON; 6. ON

EILNORT: 1. RETINOL; 2. TONIER;
3. LONER; 4. LONE; 5. ONE; 6. ON

Animal Names (page 74)

1. hippopotamus; 2. hamster; 3. lion;
4. giraffe; 5. rabbit; 6. mountain goat;
7. elephant; 8. opossum; 9. moose;
10. rhinoceros.

Answers

Elevator Words (page 74)

1. PITCHING wedge; 2. wedge heel; 3. heel bone; 4. bone china; 5. china cabinet; 6. cabinet minister; 7. minister TO

Word Ladder (page 75)

Answers may vary.
1. HALTER, falter, fatter, matter, master, faster, fasten, HASTEN
2. CRIME, grime, gripe, tripe, trope, TROVE

Word Spiral (page 75)

INTREPID, RESOLUTE

Themeless (pages 76–77)

Letter Tiles (page 77)

Answers may vary. 1. altar; 2. intro; 3. lanai; 4. natal; 5. nitro; 6. ratio; 7. talon; 8. trail; 9. train; 10. trial

Family Function (page 78)

Crypto-Wisdom (page 79)

1. Worry is a misuse of the imagination.
2. The worst thing about mistakes in the kitchen is that you usually have to eat them.
3. Do not forget that appreciation is always appreciated.

Mystery List (page 79)

Billy's typing was off by one key to the right. What he wants is a: dog, bike, skateboard, toy robot.

E Pyramid (page 80)

```
      E
     H E
    S H E
   S H E D
  S H I E D
 S H I E L D
```

Divine Intervention (page 81)

EFISTTY: 1. TESTIFY; 2. FEISTY; 3. TESTY; 4. FEST; 5. FIE; 6. IF

EHOPPRT: 1. PROPHET; 2. HOPPER; 3. OTHER; 4. POPE; 5. PHO; 6. OP

In the House? (page 82)

Mystery word: DOCTOR

```
              R
         5. O N G
        4. T A G
       3. C A R B
      2. O R D E R
     1. D I E T E R
```

A Wise Man Said It (page 82)

"Not every truth is the better for showing its face undisguised and often silence is the wisest thing for a man to heed."
– Pindar

Answers

Connections (page 83)

1. mother
2. box
3. back
4. wild
5. book

Sort and Fit (page 83)

The Loopy Lexicon (pages 84–85)

Another Word for It (page 85)

RACQUET, RACKET

Pop the Question (page 86)

AINOPSS: 1. PASSION; 2. PIANOS;
3. SPANS; 4. PAIN; 5. PIN; 6. PA

EILMOPR: 1. IMPLORE; 2. MOPIER;
3. MOPER; 4. MOPE; 5. MOP; 6. OP

Rhyme Time (page 87)

1. free me; 2. dime lime; 3. sent rent;
4. still will; 5. steer here; 6. spell well;
7. spare snare; 8. store chore; 9. quite trite;
10. normal formal

Makes a Good Dog (page 87)

KETCHUP/MUSTARD

It's All Behind You (page 88)

Word Ladder (page 89)

Answers may vary.
1. ROCK, rack, race, rice, MICE
2. YARD, card, cart, dart, DIRT
3. SOCK, lock, look, book, BOOT
4. PARK, bark, barn, born, CORN

Add-a-Letter (pages 90–91)

Balanced Letters (page 92)

3. D, E

Letter Sets (page 92)

B. The letters in group A are formed with
2 strokes; 3 strokes for group B; 4 strokes
for group C. H is formed with 3 strokes.

Honeycomb Cross (page 93)

Answers

What Castles Are Made Of (page 93)

1. chalets; 2. elastic; 3. calmest;
4. tackles; 5. scarlet

Words to Wave At (page 94)

Keep It Flowing (page 94)

WASTEWATER

Double Them Up (page 95)

Mystery word: PEDESTRIAN

Tour de Force (page 96)

DEELOPX: 1. EXPLODE; 2. ELOPED;
3. POXED; 4. PEEL; 5. OPE; 6. OX

DEILMOP: 1. IMPLODE; 2. DIMPLE;
3. MOPED; 4. POEM; 5. LOP; 6. PE

Geography Scrambler (page 97)

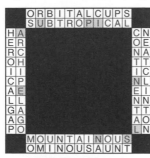

Double Rhyme (page 98)

1. big fig; 2. wee tree; 3. goat coat; 4. Acts
facts; 5. keep sheep; 6. wrong song; 7. Red
Sea plea

Wedge Words (page 98)

2 Rules (page 99)

There are two rules for ultimate success in
life. Never tell everything you know.

A Challenging Thing to Do (page 99)

Keeping your mouth shut and being tactful
may or may not be the same thing. It all
depends on your timing.

A Happy Holiday (page 100)

S ONESELF S
T GASEOUS T
O KEYLESS U
C IGNOBLE F
K SHERIFF F
I NEGLECT F
N TABLEAU R
G CALIBER S

Decorations (page 101)

ORNAMENTATION

Answers

Grid Fill [page 101]

Got Hot [page 102]

1. got hot; 2. cub snub; 3. slow flow;
4. dorm form; 5. finer liner; 6. rift shift;
7. muddy study; 8. reach beach;
9. stock shock; 10. regal eagle

Word Circle [page 102]

cellar, arouse, sequel, eleven, entice

Cast-a-Word [page 103]

1. A N P S T V; 2. B C D I M Y;
3. E H K L R X; 4. F G J O U W

Bird Words [page 103]

Across: eagle, emu, rook, swan, flamingo,
hen, crow, gull, heron
Down: jay, hornbill, dove, owl, pheasant, tit,
duck, hawk, lark

Add-a-Letter [pages 104–105]

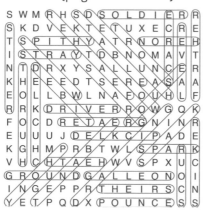

Shooting Star [page 106]

All Kinds of People [page 106]

HOMINID

Goal in Mind [page 107]

Mystery word: HOCKEY

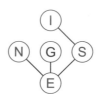

Network [page 107]

Precious Little [page 108]

ADDIMNO: 1. DIAMOND; 2. DAIMON;
3. NOMAD; 4. MAID; 5. DIM; 6. DO

AIMNRUU: 1. URANIUM; 2. RUMINA;
3. UNARM; 4. RAIN; 5. RUM; 6. UM

What to Do? [page 109]

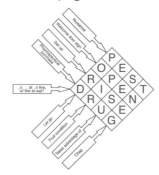

Answers

Brown Words (page 109)
LEATHER, BEAR, WALNUT

Acrostic Anagram (page 110)

A. anyway; B. arctic; C. watery;
D. tower; E. chain; F. annoys; G. ozone; H.
utility; I. heaved; J. flank; K. layout; L. vivid

"You can't say that civilization don't
advance . . . for in every war they kill you a
new way."

You Own It! (page 110)
PROPRIETOR

Word Ladder (page 111)

Answers may vary.
1. BANK, sank, sane, SAVE
2. BIRD, bind, bend, bent, best, NEST
3. EARN, darn, dare, care, case, CASH
4. WINS, tins, tine, tone, tote, VOTE

Broken Word Chain (page 111)

Word Paths (page 112)

1. Waste not, want not
2. Look before you leap

Tough Stuff (page 113)

1. free tea; 2. beer dear; 3. great mate;
4. don chiffon; 5. handbag gag;
6 cordovan fan; 7. club grub;
8.finer eyeliner; 9. griddle riddle;
10. exhorts shorts; 11. necklace place;
12. lotion devotion; 13. broadway play

Writer's Block (page 113)
AUTOBIOGRAPHICAL

Conflicting Traits (page 114)
RECKLESS, CAREFUL

Spin-o-Rama (page 114)

Word Circle (page 114)

Tenpin, invade, derive, verbal, almost,
stupor, ornate

Addagram (page 115)

1. The missing letter is T.
Target, fortnight, theater, wealth
2. The missing letter is E.
Casserole, outrage, reduce, mediocre

Full of Science
(page 116)

Can You Relate to This? (page 116)
EMPATHY

Timing Is Everything
(page 117)

Answers

Same Old Thing! (page 117)
MONOTONOUS

A Little Woolly (page 117)
LAMBKIN

Get There Safely (page 118)

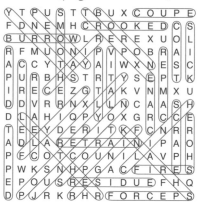

Word Ladder (page 119)
Answers may vary.
1. GOOD, gold, gild, wild, WILL
2. JELLY, belly, bells, belts, beats, BEANS
3. BIRD, bard, card, care, CAGE
4. DUCKS, dunks, dinks, kinks, KINGS

Add-a-Letter (pages 120–121)

A Word to the Wise (page 122)
A COMMON WORD

Word Jumble (page 122)
PERSONALITY

Wedge Words (page 123)

Perfect Fit (page 123)

Follow the Arrows (page 124)

To the Letter (page 124)
PLANE, PLAN

Fashionable Scramblegram (page 125)

Answers

Over and Oat (page 126)

CCHNRUY: 1. CRUNCHY; 2. CRUNCH;
3. CHURN; 4. YUCH; 5. CRY; 6. UH

AAGLNOR: 1. GRANOLA; 2. AGONAL;
3. ALONG; 4. RANG; 5. LOG; 6. LA

6-Letter Anagrams (page 127)

1. trains/strain; 2. aspire/praise;
3. secure/rescue; 4. toured/detour;
5. sister/resist; 6. hatred/thread

Take the Elevator (page 127)

1. POTATO salad; 2. salad green; 3. green olive;
4. olive pit; 5. pit stop; 6. stop short;
7. short STRAW

Letter Sudoku (page 128)

S	P	O	C	I	U	R	H	T
H	U	I	T	R	O	S	P	C
T	C	R	S	P	H	I	O	U
R	H	S	P	U	I	T	C	O
C	O	U	R	T	S	H	I	P
P	I	T	H	O	C	U	S	R
I	T	C	U	H	P	O	R	S
O	R	P	I	S	T	C	U	H
U	S	H	O	C	R	P	T	I

Letter Joust (page 128)

Mystery word: MEDIEVAL

5. B E
4. V A T
3. R A I D
2. R E V E L
1. D R A G O N

Word Ladder (page 129)

Answers may vary.
1. TRAWL, brawl, brail, grail, grain, brain, brawn, PRAWN
2. BLUNT, brunt, grunt, grant, grand, gland, bland, BRAND

Fitting Words with a P (page 129)

C	O	M	B	S
A	V	E	R	T
M	A	N	I	A
P	L	U	M	B

Overlapping Words (pages 130–131)

T	W	I	N	G	E	S	T	U
E	S	T	H	O	U	S	E	N
U	N	T	E	R	U	P	C	T
G	E	A	T	H	E	T	O	I
N	C	E	K		N	U	N	L
O	S	H	C	E	P	R	D	T
T	E	R	E	V	O	N	U	E
S	D	I	R	R	O	T	C	D
I	P	Y	T	S	A	N	Y	D

Rhyme It (page 132)

1. mad grad; 2. play day; 3. same name; 4. bite tight; 5. lame claim; 6. very hairy; 7. fair share; 8. maybe baby; 9. wrong song; 10. chief grief; 11. court sport; 12. spare chair; 13. appear near; 14. jacket racket; 15. candle scandal

A Demanding Puzzle (page 132)
INSISTENCE

What's the Catch? (page 133)

EGHINRR: 1. HERRING; 2. HINGER;
3. REIGN; 4. NIGH; 5. GHI; 6. NE

ACFHIST: 1. CATFISH; 2. FAITHS;
3. FACTS; 4. ITCH; 5. AFT; 6. IF

Answers

Grid Fill (page 134)

```
A L T E R S
S N A P P Y
H A R D L Y
S C H O O L
S T R E A K
N E E D L E
C R E D I T
```

Holiday Wordplay (page 138)

The letters A C E H I M R S T Y can be rearranged to spell CHEMISTRY: A.

Alphabet Fill-In (page 139)

1. solid	6. junta	11. clump
2. khaki	7. zilch	12. wharf
3. bayou	18. query	13. lingo
4. venom	19. egret	
5. relax	10. green	

Letter Powwow (page 139)

CONFERENCE

Animal Riddles (page 135)

1. What is black and white and "red" all over? A zebra wearing lipstick.
2. Why did the police arrest the bird? Because it was a robin.

From Soft to Hard (page 135)

SOFT, sort, sore, core, cord, card, HARD

Bowling Terms (page 136)

1. strike; 2. frame; 3. string;
4. pin; 5. alley; 6. spare; 7. ball;
8. score

Blocked In (page 140)

Letter Block Lock
(page 137)

Game On! (page 140)

```
M E G A
G A M E
A G E M
E M A G
```

Get Fit (page 137)

Before You Sip (page 141)

Rhyme Time (page 138)

1. why try; 2. stew crew; 3. rich witch;
4. time crime; 5. ford board; 6. swell bell;
7. clock lock; 8. brunch bunch; 9. clever
lever; 10. coerce verse; 11. muzzle puzzle;
12. beneath teeth; 13. never endeavor;
14. after laughter; 15. boring flooring

Answers

The Cogs of War (page 142)

AAIORTV: 1. AVIATOR; 2. VIATOR;
3. RATIO; 4. ROTI; 5. VIA; 6. AT

ACIORRS: 1. CORSAIR; 2. SCORIA;
3. ROARS; 4. ARCS; 5. CAR; 6. AS

Word Ladder (page 143)

Answers may vary.
1. FOOT, fool, foil, fail, fall, BALL;
2. SNOW, slow, slot, soot, foot, FORT;
3. SIDE, tide, tile, tale, talk, WALK;
4. LEFT, lift, lint, hint, hind, HAND

Make the Cut (page 144)

Word Pyramid (page 145)

```
  SEA
 SANE
 SNARE
RAVENS
RAVINES
INVADERS
VINEYARDS
```

A Twisted Wrister (page 145)

Wordstrain (page 146)

Word Weft (page 146)

```
T R I   P
R I D   E
I D L   E
P   E L
E   R R S
```

Musical Chairs (page 147)

AEGPSTU: 1. UPSTAGE; 2. GETUPS;
3. UPSET; 4. GUST; 5. SPA; 6. UP

CCENORT: 1. CONCERT; 2. CORNET;
3. TONER; 4. RENT; 5. TEN; 6. TE

Similar Lines (pages 148–149)

1. Fit as a fiddle;
2. Blind as a bat;
3. Clean as a whistle;
4. Light as a feather;
5. Pretty as a picture;
6. Slow as a tortoise;
7. Stubborn as a mule

Odd One Out (page 150)

HEN. All the other words can be used as verbs.

Cast-a-Word (page 150)

1. A C H K V Y
2. B M N O P U
3. D F G I R S
4. E L Q T W X

Addagram (page 151)

1. The missing letter is M.
Spaceman, hamstring, steamer, chamber
2. The missing letter is A.
Warthog, mermaid, sesame, manicure

Answers

Elevator Words (page 152)

1. QUICK study; 2. study guide; 3. guide word; 4. word processing; 5. processing time; 6. time zone; 7. zone DEFENSE

A Measure of Deception (page 152)

The best way to set a new record is to be far away from any tape measures, scales, or witnesses.

Say What? (page 153)

A revolution is an idea which has found its bayonets — Napoleon Bonaparte.

A Nice Trait to Have (page 153)

EVENHANDED

Scrambled Identity (page 154)

COSTUME

6-Letter Circles (page 154)

Carpe Diem (page 155)

AEIRTVY: 1. VARIETY; 2. VERITY; 3. TEARY; 4. ARTY; 5. TAE; 6. YA

EINORTU: 1. ROUTINE; 2. TONIER; 3. NOTER; 4. RITE; 5. ROT; 6. OR

Cast-a-Word (page 156)

1. A K L V W Z   2. B D E R S U
3. C F G I N Y   4. H J M O P T

Chomp Romp (page 156)

1. fun run; 2. cob glob; 3. grand band; 4. reach beach; 5. large barge; 6. skips chips; 7. peach speech; 8. states plates; 9. concert shirt

Sweetheart Scramble (page 157)

Grid Fill (page 158)

Shell Game (page 158)

GEODUCK

Permission Granite (page 159)

EGGLOOY: 1. GEOLOGY; 2. GOOGLY; 3. GOOEY; 4. EGGY; 5. EGG; 6. GO

EGINOSU: 1. IGNEOUS; 2. SOIGNE; 3. USING; 4. SIGN; 5. GIN; 6. GO

Fast Food (page 160)

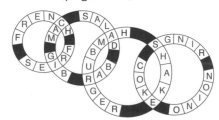

Answers

Word Jigsaw
(page 160)

Puzzle Pilgrim (page 161)

F	O	W	L	M	E	A	R	Y
L	E	A	Y	F	R	M	W	O
Y	R	M	O	A	W	L	F	E
R	F	E	A	W	Y	O	M	L
M	A	Y	F	L	O	W	E	R
O	W	L	R	E	M	F	Y	A
E	M	O	W	R	L	Y	A	F
A	L	R	M	Y	F	E	O	W
W	Y	F	E	O	A	R	L	M

Stand and Deliver
(page 161)

Mystery word: PULPIT

5. IN T
4. PIT
3. LORD
2. UNDER
1. PRIEST

Comrade Calamity (page 162)

An enemy can partly ruin a man, but it takes a good-natured injudicious friend to complete the thing and make it perfect.

Abundant S's (page 162)

		S	H	E
S	A	L	A	D
A		A		I
S	T	I	N	T
S	I	N		

Coif-Doku (page 163)

Y	A	H	E	L	T	R	I	S
S	E	L	Y	R	I	T	H	A
R	I	T	H	A	S	E	L	Y
T	Y	A	R	I	L	H	S	E
L	R	E	S	H	Y	A	T	I
H	S	I	A	T	E	Y	R	L
A	T	S	I	Y	H	L	E	R
E	L	Y	T	S	R	I	A	H
I	H	R	L	E	A	S	Y	T

Puzzle Buzzle (page 163)

1. fly high; 2. spare chair; 3. pool rule; 4. gets pets; 5. rose rows; 6. clown frown; 7. sick chick; 8. thin skin; 9. throw snow; 10. passed last; 11. mute flute; 12. cape tape

Math Scramblegram (page 164)

This Game Is Wild!
(page 164)

Mystery word: VENISON

6. IN
5. DOG
4. BUSH
3. RIFLE
2. TRAILS
1. VARMINT

Answers

Hidden Word (page 165)
NEARSIGHTEDNESS

This Will Irritate (page 165)
TENDINITIS

Add One Letter (page 166)

Step to It (page 167)

Today's Special (page 167)

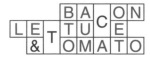

Like New (page 168)

Elevator Words (page 168)
1. JUMBO jet; 2. jet ski; 3. ski tow;
4. tow truck; 5. truck stop; 6. stop sign;
7. sign LANGUAGE

Tidbit Words (page 169)

Bingo! (page 169)
CITIZEN

Textiles (page 170)

Word Assembly (page 170)

Harmonic Convergence (page 171)
EINORTT: 1. TRITONE; 2. TONIER;
3. NOTER; 4. RITE; 5. ROT; 6. OR

ACCDEEN: 1. CADENCE; 2. ACCEDE;
3. DANCE; 4. NEED; 5. CEE; 6. DA